Festival Days

Festival Days

A History of
Jewish Celebrations

CHAIM RAPHAEL

GROVE WEIDENFELD
New York

Published by Grove Weidenfeld
A division of Grove Press, Inc.
841 Broadway
New York, NY 10003-4793

First published in Great Britain in 1990 by
George Weidenfeld & Nicolson Limited, London

Library of Congress Cataloging-in-Publication Data

Raphael, Chaim.
    Festival days: a history of Jewish celebrations/Chaim Raphael.
  —1st ed.
       p.   cm.
    Includes bibliographical references (p.   ) and index.
    ISBN 0-8021-1147-5: $19.95
    1. Fasts and feasts—Judaism.   I. Title.
BM690.R39   1990
296.4′3—dc20   90-25371
                                            CIP

Manufactured in the United States of America

Printed on acid-free paper

First American Edition 1991

10 9 8 7 6 5 4 3 2 1

*'Mo'adim l'simchah, chaggim u'zmannim
l'sason'*

'Gatherings for gladness, festival times
for joy'

From the *Kiddush* (wine blessing)
on Festival Eve

Contents

Contents

Festival Days

Introduction

The Jewish calendar includes a host of major and minor celebrations in a continuous, almost non-stop process throughout the year. Each has a distinctive character, mingling history and religion. A brief list of major occasions appears at the beginning of chapter 1, but a preliminary word may usefully bring out some general ideas on the subject as a whole.

For good reason, as we shall see, the festive calendar includes fasts as well as feasts. A great many go back in essentials to primitive times, but one must also recognize that from the beginning these occasions were constantly evolving, as they still evolve today, with new meanings, reflecting the changing circumstances of Jewish life. Even where the celebrations lean on well-established procedures going far back in tradition, the celebrants are enriching the themes, consciously or unconsciously, with feelings of their own. In this sense and others, the festival picture covers a much wider canvas than might be suggested by formal explanations.

Pursuing this, one becomes aware, in considering the festivals, that they add up to a demonstration of the uniqueness of Jewish history in the world story. In saying this, it is not being suggested that Jewish celebrants always have in mind a construct of this kind. Still less so, will the general observer look for a similar overall pattern. Most non-Jews invited to the *Seder* gathering on Passover Eve will normally be aware simply that this occasion celebrates the escape of the Jews from slavery in Egypt. Even with a thin outline of this kind for each festive day, jollity and fraternity will be forthcoming in abundance. It is only later, in the freedom of a book, that one sees how much more is available through each festival to enrich Jewish experience.

The enrichment comes partly through seeing how gaps or contradictions in traditional 'explanations' are, as it were, annealed when the Jewish background is broadened into a wider context. One still starts with traditional observance, but one is aware at the same time that this is only part of the story. To know of wide parallels intensifies one's sense of wonder at the way the Jewish ancestors drew, from a

1

common background, ideas and celebrations that became so decisively their own.

It is rewarding also to discover that within the Jewish tradition itself, celebration took forms that can vary sometimes from the received image of the festival. Here very briefly are two examples that illustrate this – one related to *Yom Kippur* (the Day of Atonement), the other to the Feast of *Purim*.

Yom Kippur normally stands for total solemnity. Its observance in synagogue today echoes in this regard the rituals carried out more than 2,000 years ago in the Temple at Jerusalem. There is a graphic account of the ancient rituals in a famous book called the *Mishnah*, which brings together laws and memories compiled by the rabbis in the century following the destruction of the Temple in 70 CE. But the *Mishnah* account (which we will draw on later) goes beyond the awesome presentation of the Temple scene on this solemn day. It reveals also that the Temple celebrations in the morning turned into a joyous gala, one of the two days of the year which expressed total happiness. To illustrate this we are told that the girls of Jerusalem, clad in white dresses, went out on *Yom Kippur* to dance in the vineyards and to call to the young men, 'Lift up your eyes, and see who you would choose for yourself.' At first this seems a little odd; but when we come to discuss *Yom Kippur* later in this book, we shall see that the detail the *Mishnah* gives us of 'dancing in the vineyards' offers a perhaps surprising idea about the origin of *Yom Kippur* itself, linking it unexpectedly to the other festivals from which it would seem so distant.

If this shows that a fast-day can be picked out as a gala, a surprise lies in wait the other way round over the celebration by some Jews of the fifteenth–seventeenth centuries of the Feast of *Purim*. *Purim* is normally a carnival, recalling the deliverance of the Jews of Persia in ancient times from a massacre being organized by the Jew-hater Haman, chamberlain to the king. The king's Jewish wife Esther averted this horror, a triumph celebrated joyously ever since. But *Purim* jollity was not the practice in one very poignant situation. The Marranos (Christianized Jews) of Spain and Portugal, who tried in most respects to keep the Jewish festivals alive secretly among themselves, turned away from the joyous side of *Purim* and concentrated instead on observing a routine (though minor) fast-day – 'the Fast of Esther' – one day earlier, commemorating her anguish at having to confront and defeat the wicked Haman. It is easy to see with hindsight why the Marranos, feeling in a parallel danger, gave up the gala to relive Esther's fast-day; but we shall discover also that feasts and fasts can be closely integrated in any case, and that this may indeed throw a new light on the ancient character of the festivals.

This is in line with what was mentioned above: that the festivals are not finite as they stand in origin and observance but have always been, and are still today, starting-points from which new forms of expression may evolve. Two examples stand out in our own time, one immensely serious relating to the Holocaust, the other a light-hearted transformation in Israel today of what had hitherto been merely a minor festival.

For the Jews in the locked-up ghettoes during the Holocaust period, doomed, as we now know, to the unspeakable bestiality of mass-murder, the day on which an ancient festival came round for 'celebration' was bitter indeed. In diaries, discovered after the war, that some of the victims kept with a religious determination to leave a record for generations to come, some kind of light is shed on how this grim situation was faced. We see in the diaries that with a festival imminent the desperate prisoners of the ghetto undertook some kind of observance of it, even though they suspected, and soon came to know for certain, that any day could signal their transportation to a death-camp. As experienced in the midst of this kind of horror, the ancient festival may have been a straw to cling to in a wholly new way, in bitterness but with some sort of belief that these holy days were still signposts to Jewish life. It was as if there was a blind, irrational feeling that Jewish history could not possibly end in a black emptiness. In this spirit they could perhaps believe that the festival days, in their vivid expression of Jewish history, could be focal points for a renewal of life. Overwhelmingly, it was a faith that was betrayed for millions of the celebrants; yet for survivors, a transformation lay in wait through the emergence of Israel, with the festivals adding a new dimension to the old pattern of celebration. This new dimension is built around the celebration of the festivals in their land of origin, uniting the celebrants with their ancestors on the same soil.

This leap across the centuries is dramatized in a different and wholly joyous spirit by the celebration in Israel today of an old folk-festival known as *Tu B'Shvat*, which occurs on the fifteenth day of the winter month *Shvat*, with *Tu* standing numerically for fifteen. In seasonal terms this festival is linked to the winter solstice, the timing being half-way through the month in which the solstice occurs. It is paralleled by a similar folk-festival for the summer solstice, held on the fifteenth day of the summer month *Av*. In ritual terms *Tu B'Shvat* signals the time when the autumn rain usually comes to an end in Israel, so that fruit trees blossoming after this time begin, so to speak, a new year. This was relevant in ancient times to the paying of tithes on the fruit, which led to the festival being called the 'New Year for Trees'. The festival itself was always very minor; but now, by an oddity of history, this popular tag has emerged with a completely new meaning, linked not only to fruit trees but to all trees. Trees have acquired an enormous new importance in Israel, in connection with the conquest of the desert, the draining of marshes and the enrichment of the soil. With this in mind, *Tu B'Shvat* has become a festival for wide celebration in new ways, particularly through giving it a special meaning for children. Tree-planting ceremonies by children everywhere – under the old-established programme of the Jewish National Fund – have given the New Year for Trees a marvellous freshness and vitality.

A dramatic turn of this kind is not the only way in which the festivals evolve in expression, even when apparently dominated by traditional ceremonies. Throughout the ages, thousands of Jews approaching the celebration of this or that festival have been moved to express their feelings in a wide range of poetry, secular as well as religious. It has added up over the centuries to a mirror of life in many lands. Some of the poetry has been used for many years in synagogue services, but some of it lay hidden for centuries and is only now being discovered. We shall see evidence of this literary development of festival feeling later in this book; and it is noteworthy that this form of Jewish expression has been particularly rich in our own time.

But the most obvious illustration of the changing emphasis in festival celebration lies, perhaps surprisingly, in the Bible itself. At one level the Bible gives us, especially in *Exodus* and *Leviticus*, very precise rules that still govern the major festival celebrations; but there are numerous references also in the Bible to earlier folk-memories, which offer hints of celebrations filling out – and sometimes apparently running counter to – the rationale of the festivals as then handed on. We shall look at this to see what light it can throw on the evolving festival scene in ancient times.

This evolution, we shall see, carries within itself the two key aspects of Jewish emergence. At one level, the ancient Hebrews were linked to the cultures around them; at another, they had been transformed by the revelation through Moses of a faith in God that enshrined a new approach to morality. It is a tribute to the Bible that it never fails to record the persistent hesitations of the Jews in fully accepting this new faith; and the evidence often lies decisively in the spirit engendered at the festivals.

To the prophets, a spiritual emptiness had invaded the festival rituals. With stirring eloquence they denounced this, telling of God's reproof in language designed to stimulate a moral renaissance. 'Bring no more vain oblations . . .', Isaiah says in God's name. 'Your new moons and your appointed feasts my soul hateth. . . . I am weary to bear them' (*Isaiah* 1:13–14).

Moral sincerity was demanded in the marvellous poetry which emerged from these denunciations. The language was fierce and archaic, but it lived on to become part of the ethical treasure of all mankind.

Part One

THE FESTIVALS
IN HISTORY

THE TRADITIONAL FESTIVALS
(with approximate timing in the secular calendar)

1 *The Pilgrim Festivals*
This general term can be used for the three major festivals which, in Bible times, had to be celebrated by a pilgrimage to Jerusalem to offer sacrifices at the Temple: Passover (*Pesach*) in April; Pentecost (*Shavuot*) in May; Tabernacles (*Sukkot*) in September/October.

2 *The Days of Awe*
New Year (*Rosh Hashanah*) in September; Day of Atonement (*Yom Kippur*) in September/October.

3 *The Patriotic Memories*
Reflecting major events in history: Feast of Dedication (*Chanukah*) in December; Festival of Lots (*Purim*) in March; Fast of *Av* (*Tisha B'Av*) in August.

4 *The Minor Celebrations*
(i) *Feasts*: New Year for Trees (*Tu B'Shvat*) in January; *Lag Ba'Omer* in May; Fifteenth of *Av* in August.
(ii) *Fasts*: Fast of Esther in March; Fast of the First-born in April; Seventeenth of *Tammuz* in July; Fast of Gedaliah in September; Tenth of *Tevet* in December.

1

The Festivals Old and New

To see the festivals in the round, we approach them in this book from three viewpoints. In Part One, we deal with some broad festival themes that transcend Jewish history as a whole. In Part Two – 'Each Festival Its Flavour' – we take the festivals one by one chronologically to form a consecutive calendar. In Part Three – The Festive Mood' – we look at the experience in two forms: first, in 'A Festival Round-about', through a brief anthology of festival 'happenings'; and then, in 'A Festival Garland', through the evocation of this experience in poetry, ancient and modern.

As a starting-point for a conspectus of the festival scene as a whole, we have set out on the opposite page a list of the traditional celebrations arranged in four groups: 1. The Pilgrim Festivals; 2. The Days of Awe; 3. The Patriotic Memories; and 4. The Minor Celebrations.

Though it is natural to start in this way with the traditional celebrations, we have to be aware from the beginning that this is not the full picture. For one thing, the traditional list does not include some important new celebrations which have emerged in Israel with a strength of feeling greater than that linked to many occasions included in the list. In this category, Independence Day (*Yom Ha'atsma'ut*), celebrated annually on the anniversary of the proclamation of the State of Israel in 1948 (the Hebrew date works out at 18 April in 1991), is a festival which can be enjoyed by many thousands who themselves took part in events now commemorated by the Jewish people as a whole. It is doubly momentous in this sense, unlike, say, the patriotic festival of *Chanukah*, which has to look so far into the past for its rationale.

9

In a wholly different mood, but with equally strong feeling, Israel has instituted a memorial day, *Yom Hashoah*, celebrated just before Independence Day, to recall the Holocaust. Here, too, there is personal involvement to be drawn on by many thousands who can never forget; yet the tragedy is felt universally and will continue to be in succeeding generations. There is a parallel here in the abiding memory for the last 2,000 years of the inexpressible sorrow which overwhelmed the Jewish people when Jerusalem and its Temple were destroyed by the Romans in 70 CE. Every Jew who has lived since then and been aware at all of history has carried this tragedy with him. The twenty-four-hour fast on its anniversary – the ninth of *Av* – is its commemoration, but the awareness goes deeper in the longing it generated for the return to Zion.

In these two new celebrations – *Yom Hashoah* and *Yom Ha'atsma'ut* – we see a reflection of the continuity expressed in festivals, sometimes for tragedy, sometimes for joy.

On a much smaller scale, but interesting in its own right, is a festival which has emerged in Israel almost by accident and which nevertheless celebrates in an unexpected way the miracle of the ingathering of Jews to the new state from countries of the Near East. Among the ancient Jewish communities of North Africa now absorbed into Israel, the Jews of Morocco had built up a festival called *Maimuna*, at which they came together for a great carnival of song, dance and marvellous food, held everywhere in Morocco shortly after Passover. When the Moroccan Jews reactivated this celebration in Israel, it soon became attractive to masses of Israeli Jews. Today it is firmly established as a much-enjoyed festive occasion bringing together political, social and artistic leaders in full enthusiastic attendance. By a parallel influence, the old custom of visiting the shrines of ancient holy men on certain days of the year, very common among Jews living in Arab countries, also seems to be more widely followed.

Even as amplified, however, this brief listing leaves out two re-current festivals in the Jewish year which dominate the background both in origin and practice. The first is the celebration of the new moon. In ancient Israel this was a festival going back to the most primitive times, but it retained its power quite remarkably as a religious festival in all the centuries which followed. A mark of its power, as we shall see, was the ruling, still operative, that the day of the new moon had to be celebrated by the recital of some of the Psalms (beginning with Psalm 113), known collectively as the *Hallel*. This was the imprimatur of official enthusiasm, not lightly granted.

Pervading the picture even more decisively is the most distinctive of Jewish celebrations, the Sabbath, so 'normal' to Jews that one might overlook its total originality as a festive way of transforming ordinary existence. The Sabbath had become a deeply embedded feature of Jewish life long before the Temple was destroyed, yet in some ways it became even more significant during the Babylonian and subsequent exiles, maintaining a pattern of life, expressed in family and communal delight, that made it, in *Galuth* ('exile') conditions, a bedrock of Jewish existence. It is noteworthy that these two pervading festivals, the Sabbath and the new moon, were closely associated in ancient observance, a hint on origins that we shall come back to.

If this listing of the festivals has conveyed the broad conspectus, we are now ready to deal in detail with the major historical themes they have expressed. The first of these is the centrality, over an immensely long time, of the idea of the pilgrimage to Jerusalem. The other abiding factor, even more ancient in origin, is the seasonal understructure of the festivals. To begin with, we shall explore this side of the festivals in terms that are embedded in the Jewish tradition; but we are able to deepen this today, drawing on archaeological discoveries, to get an understanding of ancient seasonal celebrations in many parts of the Near East, totally different in spirit from the Jewish celebrations and illuminating – we shall find – for this very reason.

The pace of archaeological discovery on this subject has been remarkably swift. It is little more than a century since the ancient Mesopotamian scene began to unfold with wholly new documentation, and this has been followed in our own day by startling discoveries in countries nearer to Israel with direct relevance to the Bible background. We shall look at some of the results later in chapter 5.

The variety that governs this wide presentation of the festival story is a response, in effect, to the endless variety of Jewish life itself. If one looks for a constant, it shows itself most decisively, perhaps, in the

11

way experience reflected in these pages comes back repeatedly to Jerusalem. We begin, then, in the next chapter, with Jerusalem, and will find the same theme dominating the end of the book, in poems included in our festival garland.

2

To Be a Pilgrim

THE FIRST PILGRIMAGE

A very far-reaching ordinance of the Bible laid down that Jews were to appear thrice-yearly at the sanctuary in Jerusalem to celebrate the festivals. The whole of Jewish history reflects a fulfilment of this pilgrimage, either in person or in spirit. Most dramatically of all, the pilgrimage to Jerusalem was the sustained stimulus which fed the Zionist drive for the return to the ancestral land. In this sense, it can be seen in some ways as the most enduring 'command' transmitted by Moses to the Jewish people.

The atmosphere of the ancient pilgrimages to the Temple at Jerusalem is reflected in marvellously evocative literature, much of it contemporary but with equal power as memories when these celebrations were being recorded in loving detail not long after the Second Temple was destroyed by the Romans in 70 CE.

Of all the literature on the pilgrimages composed while the First and Second Temples still stood, the Psalms, expressing the joy of 'going up' to Jerusalem and being in 'the court of the Lord', are as direct and moving in their power today as they must have been when first sung. Some scholars would like to interpret the familiar title *shir-hamma'lot*, which appears over a group of Psalms (120–34) and is usually rendered as 'a song of degrees', as 'a song for the ascent', referring directly to the pilgrimage. If this attractive idea is true, it is still limiting in its application; for many Psalms without this heading express the joy which the pilgrims felt in having journeyed to Jerusalem, a joy which has been kept alive – partly through these Psalms – in all succeeding generations.

One Psalm with a *shir-hamma'lot* heading (Psalm 122) certainly has a pilgrim flavour in its opening verse: 'I was glad when they said unto me, Let us go into the house of the Lord. Our feet shall stand within thy gates, O Jerusalem.' But almost at random many Psalms give us much of the same flavour even without the heading. We see a pilgrim procession evoked vividly in Psalm 68 (verse 25): 'The singers went before, the players on instruments followed after; among them were the damsels playing with timbrels.' Very explicitly there is the delight of Jerusalem in the opening of Psalm 84: 'How lovely is Thy dwelling place, O Lord of Hosts! My soul longeth, yea, even fainteth, for the courts of the Lord.' Most potent of all, perhaps, is the familiar opening of Psalm 137, in which the exiles deported to Babylon grieve for the loss of what was once so dear:

> By the rivers of Babylon, there we sat down, yea, we wept when we remembered Zion.
> We hanged our harps upon the willows in the midst thereof. . . .
> How shall we sing the Lord's song in a strange land?
> If I forget thee, O Jerusalem, let my right hand forget her cunning.

The love of Jerusalem can be felt so naturally by modern pilgrims in the Psalmist's own words – 'fair and lofty, the joy of the whole earth' – that one has to make a conscious effort to accept that in ancient times the concept of its natural beauty was heavily overlaid at festival time by an ordered increase in the system of daily Temple sacrifices that was Jerusalem's *raison d'être* in practical terms. The 'court of the Lord' was a slaughter-house of blood and fire to which all who could afford it brought their festival contribution of animals for sacrifice; and those whose means did not allow for this brought a wide range of less gory sacrifices – grain, oil, fruits, wine – to give them a sense of full participation in the rituals that were to win God's favour. From primitive times it had been fully accepted by the Hebrews (like other peoples) that the fertility on which all life depended had to be secured from the God they worshipped by offerings at set times and in set forms which brought them into direct contact with their God. Applying human standards of pleasure, they accepted the wording of the ordinances set out in *Leviticus* which spoke of the sacrifices, burning on the altar, as offering 'a pleasing odour [*re'ach nichoach*] to the Lord'. But although this was a general underlying principle in the sense that

14

God was thought to be pleased with every form of sacrifice, the variety of the occasions and the ordinances that fitted them were so vast that the meaning of the sacrifices to the participants was far more penetrating than this primitive principle would suggest.

It was this deeper meaning that made the regular Temple services, and the festival pilgrimages, so lasting in their effect. Long after the Jerusalem Temples had been destroyed, the moral imperatives in which the sacrificial system was expressed maintained the memory of Jerusalem as the undying symbol of the Jewish faith.

One seizes on this principle as a way of understanding the crucial distinction between the general pattern of sacrifices in the Near East and the form in which the Jewish pattern was expressed. If in one sense the idea of sacrificing an animal always carried with it a notion of sharing a meal with a deity, the moral implications for the ancient Hebrews were always vastly different.

One keeps this in mind when considering the fascinating theories of social anthropologists on how the whole idea of 'sacrifice' originally emerged. A common feature was always that the animal or food had to be precious to the offerer. In very primitive ages this could be the sacrifice of a first-born child; in time this was 'humanized' in various ways, such as dedicating a first-born child to the priestly service or offering first-ripe fruits. On every occasion the animal offered would have to be young and without blemish. The common feeling was, then, that the offerer earned favour as a reward for a very tangible sense of loss.

Scholars in this field have put forward a whole variety of rationales for sacrifice, ranging from offering one's own work (never a wild animal but one from one's own herd) to breaking a taboo on the consumption of something one has nurtured. Removing the 'taint' of the taboo, some explain, restored nature to its true balance and thus generated a sense of relief from danger. But if one is led into these mysterious theories to construct a rationale linked to pagan times, one is absolved from this need when one considers the moral imperatives that were set out for the Hebrews as early as the period of the Pentateuch to fit sacrifice into a moral structure.

TWO MORAL PRINCIPLES

Leaving theories on one side, it can be said that two humanistic principles stand out in the host of ordinances that are found in the book of *Leviticus*. The first, perhaps paradoxically, is the respect for life; the second is the responsibility, and also the satisfaction, of being a member of a moral community. It need hardly be said how dominant these ideas have remained in Jewish life.

The respect for life is wrapped up in the repeated statement that the life God gave to all living creatures is expressed in blood. To consume blood is therefore an offence to the sacredness of life, an offence to God. The sacrificial rituals were all framed with this in mind. If in a literal sense the ban on blood can be called a taboo, it developed in practice into an inviolate sense of respect for all humanity. The bloodthirsty rules on 'stoning to death', which survived in very ancient Pentateuchal ordinances, were totally transformed by the rabbis of the *Mishnah* when they came to frame the rules of the liberal Oral Law that the Hebrew people had lived with for generations.

We noted it as perhaps paradoxical that the sacrificial system, so full of rules for the disposing of the blood of sacrifices, should have developed under the rabbis into a legal system that bore down heavily, for humanistic reasons, on cruelty and capital punishment. It is even more paradoxical, of course, that the Jews' deep abhorrence of blood should still have allowed the promulgation in medieval Christianity of the bestial 'blood libel', in which Jews were accused of killing young children at Passover time in order to consume their blood as part of their rituals. It is hard to know what to say about this in calm terms; one simply reports it as a psycho-pathological mystery.

In suggesting above that the second underlying principle of the Jewish sacrificial system was its emphasis on the moral significance which lay at its heart, the clue has to be seen in the constant expression, set out in *Leviticus* and enjoyed by the pilgrims, that it was their sense of community which gave them the strength to work for the realization of the moral teachings of their heritage. Side by side with the communal, twice-daily animal sacrifices, with only the hide given to the officiating priest, was a major category of sacrifice called a 'sin-offering', in which the offerer brought a young animal – if he could afford it – for a ritual

16

offence. One form was a 'guilt-offering', for denying someone's legal rights. In this, as in all sacrifices, a poor person could offer two birds, or in extreme cases a small quantity of fine flour for the baking of Temple bread or wafers.

Even more explicitly in community terms, the system included 'peace-offerings' (*shelamim*) where the celebration culminated in a great communal meal, with only a small part given to the priest, and with everything else to be eaten the same day. In festival terms, we are aware of this category in the original and subsequent meals of Passover Eve. The same celebratory offerings were laid down for major community occasions, such as a victory in war or the end of a famine. A similar offering was ordered for the celebration of the *Shavuot* (Pentecost) festival.

THE HOLIDAY SPIRIT

In even more powerful terms, the sense of community was stimulated directly by rituals which generated explicit religious feelings. The excitement of the Temple scene aroused in the celebrants a palpable sense of awe – reaching a peak on *Yom Kippur* – which established a sense of communion with the God they worshipped. At another level, they were, basically, 'a people making holiday', as described not merely in the poetry of the Psalms but in historical books of the time which reflected the same excitement in more factual terms.

A vivid example of how the sense of holiday could transform the sacrificial rituals into an explosion of 'ordinary' rejoicing can be seen in the record, at a very early stage in Jerusalem's history, of how its central position was re-established in the eighth–seventh centuries BCE by two Judaean kings to a unique pre-eminence, so powerful that it has continued to reflect our current feelings. For some centuries before this restoration of centrality took place, Jerusalem's position, so strong under David and Solomon, had weakened. Under Assyrian domination, local cults had re-emerged, with sacrifices on 'every high place' and 'under every green tree'. This degeneration had been reversed only when the resolute King Hezekiah of Judah (715–687 BCE) had set out very deliberately, as part of his struggle for political independence, to destroy local cults and to centralize sacrifices in his capital, Jerusalem. A successor king, Josiah (640–609 BCE), took this transforming process further when a book of 'the Torah of Moses' (now thought to have been *Deuteronomy*) was discovered in the Temple and made the basis for a huge celebration of Passover that left its mark for all time. As recorded in the Bible (II *Kings* 23:22): 'No such Passover had been kept either when the Judges were ruling Israel or during the times of the kings of Israel and Judah.'

To redevelop the festivals in this way is an illustration of the evolutionary process mentioned earlier and due to be repeated later, always to surprising effect. Taking a long view, the biggest change came when the pattern of celebration had to be adjusted to the loss of the Temple in 70 CE, after which a synagogue service on *Yom Kippur* (see page 83) evoked the drama of Temple days, adjusted to the realities of *Galuth* life. But this major transformation of tradition was absorbed only because the destruction of the First Temple and the exile in Babylon had stimulated the growth within Jewish life of what finally emerged as 'rabbinic' leadership, creating a pattern of worship and communal loyalty that could be independent of the early sacrificial rituals.

It is relevant to note that this change in leadership came about after priestly power in Jerusalem had taken on some unappealing forms. This development had been a notable feature after the return of the Jews from Babylonian exile. The exile itself had strengthened some Jewish institutions, notably the Sabbath and the synagogue, but the Return had seen the emergence in Jerusalem of a fully articulated priestly establishment that became crucially important in the period before the Second Temple was destroyed. The contemporary record is thin for the centuries immediately following the Return; but the position is well-documented by the time the priestly leaders had turned themselves into a new dynasty of kings or king-priests – the Hasmoneans – in unholy alliance with the Syrian–Greek rulers and always suspect to the ordinary populace.

The potential conflict was obvious and all-important for subsequent Jewish history. The Hasmonean rulers had got into a powerful position by absorbing the successful military revolt against Hellenist rule led by Judah Maccabee in 168 BCE. But though this had restored the Temple to Jewish use (a victory celebrated ever after in the Feast of *Chanukah*), 'ordinary' Jews became disillusioned by the alien involvements of subsequent Jewish leaders. It was in this period that an 'alternative' leadership – becoming visible later in the teachings of the rabbis – took hold of Jewish life with a new kind of force, instilling a distinctiveness and self-confidence in Torah observance that remained for centuries at the heart of Jewish survival.

There is a paradox in this that has to be spelt out. When we first see the proto-rabbinic teachers in action after the emergence of the Hasmoneans, they are in many ways a populist opposition to the priestly-led establishment; but this never meant that they questioned in any way the religious importance of sacrifices, carried out by the priests and Levites according to the rules laid down in writing in the Torah. Indeed, they sought to deepen the impact of these rituals, and they felt that they achieved this by drawing not just on the written Torah but also on folk traditions – the Oral Torah. It was in this that a momentous rift appeared, polarizing Jewish life in the pre-Destruction period. The priestly party – known as Sadducees, from the name of an eponymous ancestor, Zadok the Priest – insisted that the priestly rule-book, as set out in the Pentateuch, was all that mattered. The 'alternative' leaders – known at first as Pharisees, from a word that meant 'separate' or 'super-observant' – argued that interpretations derived from the Oral Law, which in their view came equally from Moses, also carried authority.

The 'ordinary' Jews were ready to protest vehemently, as we shall see, if a priestly ceremony in the Temple ran foul of the customs they knew and loved; but this was very unusual, for Temple ritual was always in line with anything defined explicitly in the Torah. Immense devotion was in this way invested in Temple observance, so that even after the Temple was destroyed, the memory of its rituals remained dominant. A compelling illustration is seen in the fact that the subject-matter of the Talmud, reflecting centuries of rabbinic argument in the post-Destruction period, gives great weight to defining the sacrificial system. This preoccupation is particularly striking in the endless discussions of festival sacrifices, as if this was where the most bitter-sweet memories were expressed. It was a clear legacy also from the undying memory of the thrice-yearly pilgrimages to Jerusalem, which had been the high point of Jewish social and religious life.

The biblical law enshrining this duty had appeared originally at the most sacred point in the book of *Exodus*. Following swiftly on the Ten Commandments, God tells Moses (*Exodus* 23:17) that there are to be three festivals (which we know as Passover, Pentecost and Tabernacles) in the year and that these are to be celebrated by pilgrimages to the sanctuary: 'Three times in the year all thy males shall appear before the Lord God.' Repeated in the book of *Deuteronomy* (16:16–17), a very significant sentence is added governing the sacrifices. The festival pilgrims, we read, 'shall not appear before the Lord empty: Every man shall give as he is able, according to the blessing of the Lord thy God which he hath given thee'. The wide range of offerings for choice is set out in the book of *Leviticus* (chapter 23), as part of the general pattern of sacrificial law given there.

We have already seen how the joy of the pilgrims was reflected in many of the Psalms; but the scene is evoked much more directly in other writing available to us. Eye-witness accounts given in the books written by the Jewish-born historian, Flavius Josephus, offer interpretation as well as description of the pilgrim phenomenon. Josephus (*c.* 38–100 CE) had been a young priest in Jerusalem bearing the Hebrew name Joseph ben Mattityahu. He fought without much success as a Jewish military leader in the Roman–Jewish War, but took a 'realistic' position after the War by moving to Rome under the patronage of the emperor Titus. In this guise he wrote books that are unique in history: first, a classical account in *The Jewish War* of the fighting and its background; then a detailed and proud history of the Jewish people – *Jewish Antiquities* – which paraphrased the Bible account and took the story forward to his own time.

It is intriguing to read his explanation in *Antiquities* of why Jerusalem was turned into the only sanctuary in which sacrifices were to be held. We saw earlier that the Judaean kings Hezekiah and Josiah had brought this about as a development of their policies to fight off alien domination in politics and worship. Josephus takes the explanation back to Moses addressing his followers before his death and justifying the argument for a single sanctuary with what one might call Roman logic:

Let there be one city of the land of Canaan [Moses tells them], and this situate in the most agreeable place for its goodness, and very eminent in itself, and let it be that which God shall choose for himself, by prophetic revelation.

Let there also be one temple therein and one altar . . . and let there

20

be neither an altar, nor a temple, in any other city; for God is but one, and the nation of the Hebrews is but one. . . .

Let those who live as remote as the bounds of the land which the Hebrews shall possess, come to that city where the temple shall be, and this three times in a year, that they might give thanks to God for his benefits . . . and let them by this means maintain a friendly correspondence with one another by such meetings and feastings together.[1]

STORIES OF THE TIME

Among the many descriptions by Josephus of the tumultuous gatherings that the pilgrimages led to, one is notable in particular for presenting an unusual account of an attempt by the Roman governor Cestius Gallus (*d.* 67 CE) to have a census taken of the Jews at the current Passover celebration in Jerusalem. The method proposed was for the sacrifices to be counted and the celebrants worked out from the number reached. (There is a story in a rabbinic book of a similar census taken by a Jewish king.)

The arithmetic depended on how many celebrants came together for each paschal lamb sacrificed. We get a picture of this, of course, in the Gospels. As Josephus describes it, 'a little fraternity gathers round each sacrifice of not fewer than ten persons, and frequently as many as twenty'.[2] He tells us that the number of sacrifices counted for the census by Cestius was 255,600, which, on the basis of an average of ten persons per sacrifice, would have yielded a gathering of 2,556,000. It is, in fact, impossible that the number could have been as great as this. The historian Salo Baron says that 'the Temple could not possibly have accommodated at any time a bare fraction of that number, even if the Jews offered their sacrifices in frequent relays'.[3] Yet the numbers were undoubtedly very great, with pilgrims coming not only from all parts of Palestine, but also from the Jewish Diaspora, which was now already very widespread and totalled a vast population.

One finds echoes of this in many sources. The Jewish philosopher Philo living in Alexandria writes that 'countless multitudes from countless cities come to the Temple at every festival, some by land and others by sea, from east and west and north and south'.[4] We hear in

Acts (2:1–10) of pilgrims from many cities in Africa, Asia Minor and the Middle East amazed to hear their languages spoken, through the miraculous 'gift of tongues', when they gather in Jerusalem for Pentecost.

Babylonia, with a very large Jewish population which kept in the closest contact with the Jews of Palestine, supplied a large flow of pilgrims. Josephus mentions in one story that two Babylonian towns, Nehardea and Nisibis, used to collect the half-shekel tax for the Temple that all Jews paid, so that it could be carried safely to Jerusalem by the pilgrims: 'Many ten thousand men undertook the carriage of these donations out of fear of the ravages of the Parthians, to whom the Babylonians were then subject.'[5]

There are indications that the pilgrimages moved in organized caravans, setting off from agreed towns in Palestine and the Diaspora for the joyful journey. The adjuration to undertake the journey thrice yearly could not have meant that every individual Jew had this obligation, which would have emptied every town in the land. Rotas were doubtless arranged through the system of district representatives organized into groups known as the *Ma'amad*. There is a lively picture of this in a *Mishnah* passage describing how the First Fruits of a district were carried to Jerusalem for Pentecost, the specific festival associated with this gift to the Temple. 'How did they take up the First Fruits to Jerusalem?' the *Mishnah* asks:

> The men of the smaller towns that belonged to the *Ma'amad* gathered together in the town of the *Ma'amad* and spent the night in the open place of the town and came not into the houses; and early in the morning the officer of the *Ma'amad* said: 'Arise ye, and let us go up to Zion unto the Lord our God' (*Jeremiah* 31:6).
>
> They that were near to Jerusalem brought fresh figs and grapes and they that were far off brought dried figs and raisins. Before them went the ox (for the peace offering), having its horns overlaid with gold and a wreath of olive-leaves on its head.
>
> The flute was played before them until they drew nigh to Jerusalem. When they had drawn nigh to Jerusalem they sent messengers before them and bedecked their First Fruits. The rulers and the prefects and the treasurers of the Temple went forth to meet them. And all the craftsmen in Jerusalem used to rise up before them

and greet them, saying: 'Brethren, men of such-and-such a place, ye are welcome.'

The flute was played before them until they reached the Temple Mount. When they reached the Temple Mount, even Agrippa the king would take his basket on his shoulder and enter in as far as the Temple Court. When they reached the Temple Court, the Levites sang the song: 'I will exalt thee, O Lord, for thou has set me up and not made mine enemies to triumph over me' (Psalm 30).[6]

As against this joyful picture, the presence of large crowds often led to disturbances. In the lead-up to the War, riots would break out, with the Roman military taking stern measures. Equally, the Jews could get excited over their own quarrels. One famous incident was the occasion during a Tabernacles sacrifice, as described by Josephus, when King Alexander Yannai (*c.* 126–76 BCE), officiating in the Temple as High Priest, deliberately flouted an Oral Law custom which enjoined the pouring of water on the altar and, instead, poured it contemptuously over his feet.[7] As it was Tabernacles, the crowd were all carrying the citrons called for on this festival and pelted the king with them. At this, Josephus says,

> he was in a rage, and slew of them about six thousand. He also built a partition wall of wood around the altar and the Temple, as far as that partition within which it was only lawful for the priests to enter, and by this means he obstructed the multitude from coming at him.

Other memories were much more agreeable. In rabbinic accounts, the pilgrims stayed for the whole duration of Passover (seven days) and Tabernacles (eight days), and all found room, either in tents they pitched outside the Temple (mentioned also by Josephus) or with local residents. Because Jerusalem was seen as belonging to the whole of the Jewish people, the residents were forbidden to take rent, but were happy to receive as gifts the hides of sacrificed animals. No one, says one rabbinic book, ever had occasion to say to his neighbour: 'I have been unable to find a stove for cooking the Paschal lamb in Jerusalem, or unable to find a bed to sleep in.' A list of 'ten wonders' experienced by the pilgrims, as recorded in 'Sayings of the Fathers', says that the meat in the Temple never went putrid, no fly was ever seen in the slaughter-house, and no serpent or scorpion ever did harm in

Jerusalem. Other 'wonders', equally unreal, follow; but it is the tenth wonder which stays in the mind for its description, in the form of a brilliantly terse epigram – four words in Hebrew – of the awesome moment in the Temple on *Yom Kippur* when the assembled worshippers prostrated themselves in prayer. The signal came when the High Priest, as a culmination of immensely long rituals, entered the Holy of Holies and uttered the ineffable name of God. The moment of prostration was experienced as an astonishing 'wonder' among the tightly wedged worshippers. The epigram says it all: 'Standing – packed; prostrate – with room to spare.'[8]

THE HOLY OF HOLIES

It is a mark of Jewish faith that the sense of wonder could ultimately take over throughout history, outweighing the despair that might otherwise have risen to the surface. With this in mind, one understands the role of the festivals in sustaining Jewish life throughout the long *Galuth*. Hope for the future always lay in wait in a Bible verse; but at festival time, words were found in poetry and prayer that had a double intensity. The festivals transformed life. If, after the Destruction, the joys of the ancient pilgrimages were, for the time being, no longer possible, one dreamed of when they would be: 'Next Year in Jerusalem!' Today the wonder is fulfilled, with hosts of pilgrims once more in Jerusalem to celebrate festival time.

The emergence of modern Israel was fashioned from the love of Zion that never lost its vitality even when wholly unreal in practical terms. One heard it at every meal in the simple words of the Grace: 'O build Jerusalem the Holy City speedily in our days.' The Spanish–Jewish poet Judah Ha-Levi was ready to surrender all the bounty of Spain for a sight of the desolate shrine. Nor was the feeling merely nostalgia for what had been lost. While the Temple still stood, many a writer matched the rapture of the Psalmist. One sees this in the work of Simeon ben Sira, who lived early in the second century BCE.

Ben Sira, widely known for the forty-fourth chapter of his book *Wisdom* which begins with the oft-recited words: 'Let us now praise famous men . . .', was basically a quiet philosopher-moralist; but the sight of the High Priest emerging from the Holy of Holies on the Day of

Atonement stimulated feelings that were to echo among Jews throughout the centuries which followed:

> How glorious he was as he looked out from the Tent of the Presence, as
> he emerged from the curtained shrine! Like a star shining through the
> clouds, or the full moon on feast-days; like the sun glittering on the
> King's palace or the rainbow seen in the cloud . . . like a spreading
> olive-tree laden with fruit, or an oleaster whose branches drink their
> fill . . .[9]

It was a style of writing that was to be echoed in the festival poems
that began to be written in the Land of Israel within a few short
centuries of the Destruction, finding a beloved place in the festival
prayer-books.

In the writing of the same early period one can see how the sense of
desolation could always be dispelled if the right words were found to
express the certainties of their faith. There would be no bridle on
lamentation, but equally no disposition to accept that the Jewish story
would always be dominated by grief.

This double view emerges to powerful effect in a famous anthology of
rabbinic sayings known as the *Midrash* (commentary) on the book of
Lamentations. *Lamentations* (popularly ascribed to the prophet Jeremiah)
is an elegy for the First Temple, destroyed by Nebuchadnezzar in 586
BCE. Reading it provided the perfect atmosphere for the survivors of the
second Destruction, who expounded the text word by word to recall the
horrors that had befallen them. Yet even in this record of grief, they tell
joyful stories, when they can, to offset the persistent sorrow. For
example, one passage brings out the way the great Rabbi Akiba, who
lived through the Destruction, could reach out for hope.

The anecdote they tell has Akiba indulging in cheerful verse-play in
relation to verse 18 of chapter 5 of *Lamentations*: '*For the mountain of Zion is
desolate.*' Akiba, they tell us, was on his way to Jerusalem one day with
three rabbi companions from the academy of B'nei B'rak, where they all
taught. They got their first shocking view of what had been the Temple
when they reached Mount Scopus. They moved on, the *Midrash* says,

> and when they reached the Temple Mount, they saw a fox run out
> from the Holy of Holies. All began to weep save Akiba, who laughed.
> They said to him: Akiba! You always surprise us. We weep, and you

laugh. He said to them: Why do you weep? Should we not weep, they replied, when a fox runs out, fulfilling the verse: '*For the mountain of Zion is desolate, the foxes walk upon it*'? Akiba replied: That is exactly why I laugh.[10]

He then proceeds, with a witty demonstration of dialectical skill, to offer proof from other verses of the Bible that a series of linked prophecies, which ultimately came true, ends with a verse from *Zechariah* (8:5): '*And the streets of the city shall be full of boys and girls playing.*' I rejoice, he says, that the words of the other prophets have been fulfilled, for now the words of Zechariah will ultimately be fulfilled too. Hearing these words, they said to him: 'Akiba! You have comforted us. May you be comforted by the steps of him that brings good tidings.'

Against the many passages in the *Midrash* which display unmitigated grief, the cheerfulness of Akiba's reply is repeatedly matched by a sense of happiness at being able to tell each other stories of former greatness. Jerusalem, one hears, was a city of twenty-four major highways, leading into open places, squares, courts and clusters of houses, 'with every court housing twice as many people as came out of Egypt'. An illustration of the huge population is offered in an anecdote evoking the atmosphere of the trading caravans. One such caravan coming from Tyre was composed of 200 camels carrying an immense load of pepper for the needs of Jerusalem; but after the caravan arrived, the pepper was snatched up instantly in so many small amounts for each home that none was left for a man who was giving a big banquet that night.

The huge scale of Temple needs was adapted easily into these fancy-free tales. There were two cedars on the Royal Mount, under one of which were forty shops selling articles for the Temple rituals. The providers of goods in other towns could not keep pace with the needs of the pilgrims. Magdela of Sabarya had 300 shops selling birds for ritual purposes. There were 300 shops of weavers of cloth for cloaks in K'far Nimrah. With all this commercial activity centred on the needs of Jerusalem, it is no surprise to learn of a bank – described as an 'Arch of Accounts' – outside the city so that those making payments could do this outside the walls 'and not go about Jerusalem worrying'. Nothing was allowed to interfere with the Psalmist's description of Jerusalem as 'the joy of all the earth'.

FESTIVAL CONTINUITIES

Even without Temple sacrifice as the focal point, all the festivals in the calendar were still carried out scrupulously, following the detail set out in the *Mishnah* to establish the correct procedures. Often the logic employed to link traditional practices to the Bible text might seem hidebound, but one recognizes at the same time that a wonderful kind of good humour permeated the arguments deployed.

Examples show up on every page of the *Mishnah*, such as the mention at one point of the problem that could arise in fulfilling the ruling that, throughout the first seven days of *Sukkot*, a man must make the *Sukkah* his regular abode, using his house only if *Sukkah* occupation becomes really impossible through rain. But how does one know at what point to apply the rain test? Quite simple: 'when porridge in the *Sukkah* would be spoilt'.[11]

In another part of the *Mishnah*, the rabbis pick up this rain point to show how the festivals enable one to get a quick guide on whether God is satisfied with one's behaviour. This guide is available, they said, four times in the year: at Passover, through the ripening of the grain; at Pentecost, through the ripening of the fruit; at New Year, when a human's survival or death is weighed up by God; and at *Sukkot*, 'if it rains'.[12] God would only make life difficult for his faithful Jews if He was really angry with them!

At first it seems rather forced for the *Mishnah* to link practicalities to festival observance in this way, but we have witnessed in our own time, through the marvels of archaeology, how feelings transmitted for centuries by tradition are often given a new kind of demonstration in visible form. There is a striking example in a document discovered only a few years ago showing how Bar Kokhba, heroic leader of the last revolt against the Romans in 132–5 CE, made sure at a critical moment of the fighting that his soldiers could carry out the *Sukkot* rituals.

The epoch-making discovery of letters sent by Bar Kokhba to his officers in the field was made shortly after the foundation of the State of Israel in 1948, when the letters were first unearthed in caves near the Dead Sea. Until these letters emerged, the stories of Bar Kokhba leading a last revolt against Roman rule seemed half-legendary; but now he came to life in letters, which revealed his real name, Simeon bar

Kosiba, and gave clear instructions on military affairs and supplies. In one of these letters, discovered in a cave in 1961 by the brilliant archaeologist Yigael Yadin, Bar Kokhba gives strict instructions for the 'four plants' used in the *Sukkot* services to be sent to him. The date shows that the revolt was almost over, but he still goes to great trouble to ensure that the services will be held properly:

> Simeon to Yehudah bar Menashe in Qiryath 'Arabaya: I have sent to you two donkeys that you shall send with them two men to Yehonathan bar Be'ayan and to Masabala in order that they shall pack and send to the camp, towards you, palm branches and citrons. And you, from your place, send others who will bring you myrtles and willows. See that they are tithed and send them to the camp. The request is made since the army is big. Be well.[13]

If ever the continuity of Jewish life needed to be demonstrated, it lies in a letter like this. Festival observance would be the key to survival even when the splendour of the ancient celebrations in Jerusalem itself came to an end, and remained beyond the reach of Jews there for centuries to come.

3

The Pilgrimage Lives On

UNCERTAINTIES IN JERUSALEM

With Jerusalem and its Temple destroyed, Jewish existence had to find new ways of living out the festivals on which it had been nourished. To some extent this was not as critical a break as it might sound, since Jewish life had already taken root in many countries, with rituals fully established in *Galuth* style. But these rituals had drawn authority from an awareness of the centrality of Jerusalem. It was not always easy to keep this idea alive when the realities of existence in the ancestral land offered a desperate picture, in many centuries, of poverty and persecution. The ingredient that had to be drawn on was an unshakeable faith that one day, in a form as yet unknown, the dream of a free life in the Homeland would become a reality. To become pilgrims again, in whatever form, was part of the dream.

In the immediate shadow of the defeat by the Romans in 70 CE, it seemed at first impossible that Jerusalem, the focal point of the dream, could ever again play its ancient role. In capturing Jerusalem, the Romans had destroyed it completely, with only some remains of the Western Wall and three Herodian towers left in existence as defence points. For the ensuing sixty years, the site was deserted and used only as an encampment for the Roman forces. It was not until 132 CE that the emperor Hadrian began to rebuild the site as a Roman colony, known as Aelia Capitolina in tribute to his family name. The plan, built around new main and subsidiary roads in Roman style, included statues, a Forum and temples to Jupiter and Venus.

The rebuilding of Jerusalem as a Roman city may have been a factor

29

in the outbreak of Bar Kokhba's revolt, which began at this time and lasted for three years. It was a heroic – if doomed – struggle, with a very painful outcome for the Jews. Hadrian had already made Torah teaching a capital offence, with many rabbis – including the famed Akiba – burnt at the stake because of their defiance of the ban. In the same spirit, he barred Jews from entering the city built on Jerusalem's site. Even though there is some evidence that total exclusion was relaxed after a while, there was clearly nothing for a long time to come that could evoke for Jews the festival exhilaration that Jerusalem had once offered.

A further bar to Jewish enjoyment of their ancient capital was the growth there, from the third century on, of a strong Christian presence. When the emperor Constantine formally recognized Christianity in 313 and organized the spread of the faith throughout the empire, Jerusalem soon became a dominant Christian centre. As a result, Jews managing to live there were in a very uncertain position, a status that persisted until the whole of Palestine was conquered by the advancing Arab armies, championing the new Muslim faith, in the early decades of the seventh century.

BASIS FOR REVIVAL

Before this, however, Jewish identity had found new centres elsewhere. An important factor in Israel itself even under the Romans had been the remarkable authority enjoyed by the rabbinic leader of the second century, Rabbi Judah Ha-Nasi (Judah the Prince). Judah, born *c.*135, was a member of the family descended from the famous rabbinic teacher Hillel, and was himself a man of independent means and profound learning. Under the Roman dynasty founded in the second century by the emperor Septimus Severus, the Jews had been allowed to establish something like self-government under Judah's leadership. There are many stories in rabbinic writings of the close personal relations that existed between Judah and the authorities, often told in terms of 'theological' arguments between the rabbi and 'the emperor'. If some of these stories have the air of legend, it is a fact that Judah, as 'Prince' of the Jews, lived in considerable style. Financial support flowed in to him from the populous Diaspora. It was Judah who brought together the whole corpus of rabbinic teaching into the

Mishnah, which we have been quoting. Torah study and education flourished under the guidance of Judah's successive academies in Galilee. In this setting, which seemed for a time quite assured, new cities and lavishly decorated synagogues were built, as we know from excavations in Galilee in our own time.

A more lasting assurance came from Babylon. The decline due to Christianity had set in not merely in Jerusalem (as noted above) but throughout the Land of Israel; for though Judaism was not declared illegal by the Roman authorities, Christian contempt and hostility established the dominant pattern. By the third century, it is true, the rabbinic leadership under Judah Ha-Nasi had established a framework in the *Mishnah* that was to be of untold value in maintaining Jewish unity; but this would have had little lasting effect had there not developed to the east, in Babylon, a Jewish religious structure that had long enjoyed great respect, second in status only to Israel, which was now able to assume direct world leadership when this position faltered in Israel itself.

The leadership increasingly exercised in Babylon had had its roots in the first Exile there. The Jews weeping by the waters of Babylon, as in the famous Psalm, had certainly felt an immeasurable sense of loss at being so distant from Jerusalem, but this had not prevented them from creating a cultural life that survived, and developed further, when many of the exiles preferred not to join the Return to the ancestral land in the fourth century BCE under the leadership of Ezra and Nehemiah. It was typical of their deep Jewish feeling that the community which stayed behind developed the strongest links with the rabbis of Israel. In due course, their scholars went to study in Israel: Hillel, for example, was a Babylonian Jew by birth. Eventually, the academies of both countries were exchanging scholars freely, so that when the position of Jews in Israel lost its strength through the growth of Christianity, Babylon was able to step in.

From the very beginning, Babylonian Jewry developed a distinctive style, both socially and religiously; but a new dimension was added when the emergence of Islam in the seventh century raised the level of life generally in all Muslim lands. It had always been a mark of the Jewish community that their leader in Babylon, who bore the title of *Resh Galutha* ('Head of Exile'), was regarded as a lineal descendant of King David. With the growth of Arab power from its adopted base in

Babylon, the Jewish community itself enjoyed a new kind of splendour, expressed both in economic prosperity and in the rabbinic authority that was now centred here for centuries.

This historic change is reflected in the ensuing story of pilgrimages to the Near East. The undying love for the ancestral land still exerted its pull, but the pilgrims who have left a record of visits there found the land – and especially Jerusalem – in a sorry state.

Nothing, perhaps, could match the dreams they had nourished, expressed with particular love in the poetry of the festivals. Judah Ha-Levi, who set out from Spain in the year 1140 to see with his own eyes the visions of Zion he had conjured up in his poetry, never got further, it now seems, than Egypt. He may well have been spared a bitter disappointment, as we can judge from the experience of the great philosopher Maimonides, who managed to arrive in the land not long after Judah Ha-Levi had set out. Maimonides, who had been born in Cordoba and spent his early years in Spain, had fled with his parents and family to Morocco to escape persecution by fanatical Muslims. Fired by the love of Zion that all shared, he had undertaken a hazardous journey to the Land of Israel in 1165, but found life impossible for Jews in the struggle between the Crusaders (now in power there) and the Arabs. Judah Ha-Levi had expressed the same feeling: 'Ishmael (Islam) pursues us with his hate; we turn pleading to Esau (Christianity) and he tears us like a wild beast.'[14] After some months in Acre and a visit to Jerusalem to pray at the site of the Temple, Maimonides made his way to Egypt, where he settled down to write his books and to work as a doctor.

THE LATER PILGRIMS

The picture is equally bleak in the diary kept by the Spanish-Jewish traveller Benjamin of Tudela, who arrived in Jerusalem around 1170 after three years of travel and could only say of the current Jewish position: 'The dyeing-house is rented by the year, and the exclusive privilege of dyeing is purchased from the king by the Jews of Jerusalem.' But if, like other pilgrims for the next century or so, the contrast is always made between the bleakness of the Holy Land at this time and the luxury enjoyed by Jews in Baghdad, everything gives way to devotion when they write of the essence of the pilgrimage: the visit to the holy sites, in which Hebron almost matched Jerusalem for sanctity.

In due course, as Jews found their feet in European countries and gave wider expression to the tradition they bore with them, the pilgrim writings could evoke more direct echoes of the feeling seen in the Bible itself and in the creative periods of rabbinic Judaism which followed. Much depended, of course, on the character of the background from which the pilgrims came. The Jews of Italy, in particular, gave evidence of this in records which have come down to us. One sees this to perfection in a long, sophisticated letter written by a scholar-pilgrim from Italy in 1488, giving his father at home a realistic but still enchanting picture of the appeal of the land.[15]

The writer, Obadiah of Bertinoro, author of a well-known commentary on the *Mishnah*, describes months of travel in which he was able to enjoy the hospitality of many Jewish communities in the lands he visited en route. Inevitably, he expresses mixed feelings on finally arriving in Jerusalem, having passed through Gaza, Hebron and Bethlehem before getting his first sight of the former sanctuary.

Memories had been stirred everywhere. In Gaza he had been shown ruins said locally to be of the building that Samson pulled down on the Philistines. In Hebron he and his companions had prayed at the graves of the patriarchs. En route to Bethlehem they came to a round, vaulted building known as Rachel's tomb, where again they dismounted from their asses and prayed, 'each according to his ability'. Moving on to Jerusalem, the whole way was full of vineyards and orchards, the vines reminiscent of those in Romagna, 'low but thick'. And soon now,

we beheld the city of our delight, and here we rent our garments, as was our duty. A little further on, the sanctuary, the desolate house of our splendour, became visible, and at the sight of it we again made rents in our garments.

The synagogue he attends, he tells his father, is well run. With the wheat harvest over, the famine is at an end. The Arabs are friendly. The city, despite its destruction, 'still contains four very beautiful long bazaars, such as I have never before seen, at the foot of Zion. They all have domed-shaped roofs, and contain wares of every kind.' For the rest, there are long accounts of the varied origins of the Jews living in Jerusalem, with ideas on how their condition might be eased.

The beneficent tone of the letter puts one in mind, to some extent, of the attitude displayed a few centuries later by the great philanthropist Sir Moses Montefiore, whose determination to help the Jews of the Near East led him to make seven pilgrimages to the Holy Land, the first in 1827. There was certainly a difference in style, with Sir Moses carrying letters from Queen Victoria and being transported by ships of the Royal Navy. Yet in many ways it was a natural progression from Obadiah and the many thousands of pilgrims or settlers like him for whom the memory of Zion would never fade.

Only in our own time has there been a sea-change which one has to note. The pilgrim-drive remains basically the same for the myriads who come as tourists, but it is very different for those who live in Israel and have renewed the direct involvement, in language and rootedness, that a Jew felt there when the Temple still stood. If in physical terms life in Israel is now 'modern' by the ordinary tests of comfort and convenience, the *thought* of an Israeli is conditioned by his presence on this soil, expressed not just through politics, which is obvious, but in the shaping of personal feeling, and most evocatively in poetry.

It is in poetry that the ordinary calendar of life finds its most stirring reinterpretation, so that we are not surprised to find the festivals coming to life in new ways through the poetry of Israel. This is supremely true of the poetry of Yehuda Amichai, as can be seen in one of his poems which begins with the line: 'My Mother died on *Shavuot* when they finished counting the *Omer*.'

At one level, this first line tells us of an intimate moment in the poet's own life; but in seeing the moment identified in terms of the festival and one of its rituals, we are instantly aware of the wider dimension. As the poem moves on, the story of his mother's life becomes the story of Israel. Everything in his memory is history, but history at its most personal, springing from this soil and no other. Where she is buried was once a botanical garden, with the flowers riotous in colour and names – 'Forget-me-not, forget.'

We hear Amichai's voice, but it is a poem written for all of us. In this book it takes pride of place (on page 122) in the flowers gathered together as our festival garland.

4

The Seasonal Understructure

THE DOMINANCE OF THE HARVEST

Before we look at each festival individually in Part Two, we must spend some time with the second broad theme: the pervading importance of the seasons in the origins of the festival calendar. We are aware of this in our own celebrations today, where every festival still has a seasonal tang, but there is a wider significance, which we will examine in this and the next chapter.

If one goes behind the historical stories to look for festival origins in the celebration of the seasons, it is not to question or change the observances that have come down to us, but precisely the opposite: to enrich one's response to the traditional picture through an awareness of what originally lay behind it. One catches many glimpses in the Bible story of this earlier background, and wants to see how this may have been transmuted.

The Bible lets us see that long before a fixed pattern of worship through sacrifices was established for the festivals, the ancestors of the Jews celebrated all major occasions – such as land purchases, treaties and episodes in their pastoral and social life – with shared meals solemnized by sacrifices to the gods of the parties; and this was certainly true of the celebration of the seasons. When we read early detailed instructions on the festival sacrifices, as in chapter 23 of *Leviticus*, the celebration is usually, though not always, linked to an important event in history, but at the same time the seasonal emphasis is unmistakable. With Passover, the date is spring, highlighted as being in the first month, *Nisan*. The major sacrifice of this festival looks back in its name, *Pesach*, to the great communal meal described in the Bible as having taken place on the eve of the Exodus from Egypt; but it is not difficult to see this historic occasion as echoing also the regular spring gathering of a pastoral people that Moses spoke of in his plea to Pharaoh, a regular festival in the wilderness that he said was sacred to the Hebrews. The alternative name of the festival, 'the Feast of Unleavened Bread' (*matzah*), is also linked, of course, to the Exodus; but, in fact, baking and eating unleavened bread around the roasting lamb was routine among pastoral people.

We get an even more direct description of Passover as essentially seasonal in an instruction that the full celebration of the festival (once the Hebrew people are settled in their new home) is to include a daily '*Omer*', the offering of a sheaf of the new grain harvest (barley), starting on the second day. This sheaf will be 'waved' daily by the priest for seven weeks.

These seven weeks will have brought Israel to *Shavuot*, the Feast of Weeks (Pentecost). This will be a one-day festival, which the priest will celebrate by 'waving' two loaves of bread made from the new wheat to accompany his 'wave offering' of the animal sacrifices of the day. One notes that in the mention of *Shavuot*, nothing is said of it being the anniversary of Moses receiving the Ten Commandments on Mount Sinai, now in the forefront of the traditional image of this festival.

There is the same uneven picture in the *Leviticus* list of the celebrations of *Sukkot*, which, incidentally, is better translated as 'Booths' (country huts) rather than 'Tabernacles'. *Sukkot*, given a date in the autumn, is defined as the great harvest feast, the *Chag* (festival) *par excellence*, 'when ye have gathered in the fruit of the land'. Very appropriately for a harvest festival, the Bible specifies that four kinds of branches and fruit are to be part of the celebration. The historical reason for living in booths for the duration of the festival is, of course, mentioned, but only briefly, almost as an aside. It was obviously part of the harvest activity, but is given a 'patriotic' meaning to remind the celebrants of the wanderings in the Wilderness.

That this feature is mentioned so briefly has never prevented Jews from seeing time spent in a *Sukkah* as a major aspect of the festival, confirming what one knows historically: that all the festivals acquired their own momentum. There is an even more striking development process visible over the account in *Leviticus* of *Rosh Hashanah*. The Bible instruction asks merely for a celebration of the first day of the seventh month (*Tishri*, the month of *Sukkot*) as a formal rest-day from work, saying that there is to be 'a holy convocation' with 'a memorial of blowing of trumpets'. Nothing is said of it being the formal New Year's Day, key to the fateful position it subsequently assumed in the Jewish religious calendar as a day of judgement and fate for the year ahead.

SOLEMNITY BEFORE THE *CHAG*

By contrast, the Day of Atonement (*Yom Kippur*: more correctly *Yom ha-Kippurim*) appears with full solemnity even at this early stage. There is no specific reference to a fast, which was deduced later to flow from the phrase: 'Ye shall afflict your souls'; but 'affliction', linked to an extremely fierce prohibition of any kind of work on this day, is to apply to everyone, with a dread penalty for infringement. As it happens, the most awesome ceremony of *Yom Kippur*, when the High Priest was to enter the Holy of Holies, is not mentioned in this particular listing but in an earlier passage in *Leviticus* (chapter 16), in the context of purifying the Temple after an offence by the High Priest's sons which had desecrated it; but even without this, the concept of sin and atonement on this, the holiest day of the year, is very clearly shown.

It is all very familiar to us today, yet even with its deep religious purpose foreshadowed so positively, one can still wonder if its date in the calendar also has some seasonal significance. Like *Rosh Hashanah* nine days earlier, *Yom Kippur* is not accompanied by any historical 'explanation', but is simply a command by God, transmitted by Moses, to hold the celebration on this particular day. Yet if, in the primitive world, the celebration of the seasons is a dominant driving force, one is drawn into seeing the date of these two important celebrations as linked somehow to the great seasonal festival *Sukkot*, which follows five days after *Yom Kippur*. This indeed is how this twenty-two-day festive period of *Rosh Hashanah*, *Yom Kippur* and *Sukkot* is experienced in Jewish tradition. Individually, each of these three major occasions has become encrusted with distinctive meanings and rituals. Indeed, every single

38

day of the whole period has an individual flavour, with different moods sometimes related even to changes in the hour of the day, as, say, the feeling of resignation when night falls for the closing service of *Yom Kippur*, which became known for this reason as *Ne'ilah*, 'the closing [of the gates]'. Yet despite all these variations, there is one overall significance, turning the period into a unified drama. The themes are man in Nature, man in relation to the forces which influence his fate, an individual in moral decision, a celebrant with his own people of what is absolute in their heritage.

Taking this view, the Days of Awe are as seasonal as *Sukkot* itself, preparing the ground in an integrated way for the full celebration of life at the *Chag* which is to follow. Preparation for a great religious event is very common in Jewish life. Both *Rosh Hashanah* and *Yom Kippur* have their own preparatory periods and, taking the process further, both lead now to the celebration of the *Chag*. If one were giving these occasions summary titles, they might be Renewal for *Rosh Hashanah*, Purification for *Yom Kippur*, to culminate in Rejoicing for *Sukkot*. But this would be too rigid a pattern, for the moods of each occasion overlap. The talk of trumpets and the sound of the *shofar* (the ancient trumpet fashioned from an animal's horn) on *Rosh Hashanah* generates as much excitement as the repeated processions around the synagogue which, as we shall see, take place on *Sukkot*. If solemnity is paramount on *Yom Kippur*, the unbroken hours spent in the synagogue offer the pleasure of communal fellowship, which is so tangible a few days later when the celebrants sit together in the *Sukkah*. And on *Sukkot* itself, the joyousness of the seven-day festival gives way, when it ends, to a supplementary eighth day of utter solemnity (*shemini atsereth*), on which the congregants wear again in synagogue the white *kittel* (robe) which is the custom for the Days of Awe.

In this approach, with *Sukkot* as the final phase of a unified celebration of God's sustaining power in human existence, we are led into what otherwise needs some explanation: that *Rosh Hashanah* celebrates Creation itself. A brief *Rosh Hashanah* hymn says just this: 'Today the world is born.' In the Jewish tradition, this basic form of worship finds expression in a special prayer every morning, thanking God that one has come back to life. It is in the same spirit that the autumn season, ending the sterility of summer drought, turns to the new agricultural year. The fertility cycle which sustains human existence needs to be renewed each year. Among primitive peoples, this was more than a symbolic renewal. The universe was felt to be actually recreated at New Year, after a struggle in which the god of fertility won a battle for mastery over the destructive gods who would prevent it.

PAGAN MYTHS TRANSFORMED

This story of an ancient battle to ensure fertility was the common theme (in various forms) of all the pagan peoples of the Near East. It is only in relatively recent times that archaeology has provided details of the myths which enshrined these stories and were read out at New Year celebrations with great authority. We are therefore aware now from contemporary sources of the dominant pagan ideas, centring on control of the universe by pantheons of quasi-human gods, against which the Bible concept of a single all-powerful Being, indefinable in any kind of human terms, stands out so clearly. Everything revealed by archaeology establishes the unique force of the revolution – or Revelation – conveyed by the Bible. Yet the Hebrews were in contact with the peoples around them, and susceptible in particular to Assyrio-Babylonian, Egyptian and Canaanite influences. How much of these, one would like to know, left their mark on the Jewish traditions which were later to find expression in the festivals and their concomitant literature?

In festival worship itself, the Jewish themes were utterly different, and not only because of the admixture of national colouring that became such a prominent feature. At New Year, for example, the issue for the Jews was the moral regeneration of every individual, without which life on earth failed of its true purpose. Repentance and prayer reinforced the good life, and in this sense man was master of his own fate. But the drive for the good life was part of a communal will. It lived and was constantly refreshed in the truths that had come to the ancestors, and was expressed in the continued existence of the Jewish people. For this reason a Jew was repeatedly aware of the patriarchs in his prayers, not as mediators, but as fellow-worshippers, trembling for the sanctity of life. The rebirth of life at the autumn season was a fateful moment of human existence, with every individual's life in peril. In this setting, a Jew could be very close to the Creator.

The transformation from the pagan world of myth to the concepts that have come down to us as Jewish can be epitomized in one teaching that overflows with religious importance: the worship of God as 'King'.

Unless one looks at this closely, it can seem just poetic and sentimental. Jews are so used to the ancient prayers which begin with the words '*avinu malkenu*' – 'our Father, our King' – that nothing dramatic seems implied. But the ancient rabbis thought otherwise; and for this reason they ordered that of three themes to be spelt out repeatedly on *Rosh Hashanah*, pride of place had to be given to that of '*malchuyyot*', God as King (*melekh*).

There is something of a puzzle here, for the Bible itself never apostrophizes God as King. A glance at the festival instructions in *Leviticus* (chapter 23) mentioned earlier brings this out very clearly. The festival we know as *Rosh Hashanah*, and which is prescribed for the first day of the seventh month, *Tishri*, is not called New Year but just 'a convocation', a rest-day which is 'a memorial proclaimed with the blowing of trumpets'. Here are two of the three themes which the rabbis identified: *zichronot* (memory) and *shofrot* (trumpets). If the rabbis added – and gave pride of place to – the theme of kingship, it must have been for a very specific reason.

It is a fair speculation that a dominant purpose may have been to rebut the idea that the so-called 'kings' who had emerged in the Hasmonean dynasty in the two centuries before the destruction of the Temple in 70 CE were in any true sense 'kings' in the Bible tradition. They were, in fact, Roman puppets; and though on occasion they might stand up for the Jews (as recorded by Josephus), they had none of the holy authority which was embodied in a true descent from David. In addition to this, they had amalgamated their role with that of High Priest, in concert with the Sadducees. This was a constant offence to the Pharisees, guardians of Oral Law folk-traditions, who had been taking on teaching authority with the honorific title of 'rabbi' (Master).

Though the rabbis were growing in number and strengthening their position during this period, they were rarely able to challenge the secular power of the 'kings' or 'king-priests', and must have determined to proclaim their view in the only way open to them, by emphasizing that God alone is King. There is, in fact, a passage in the Talmud which says this explicitly, quoting a rabbi who says that God Himself ordained the kingship theme on *Rosh Hashanah* to emphasize that He alone is King.[16]

As a further illustration of the religious passion over the use of this term, one need look only at the tremendous conflict which broke out when the mad emperor Caligula demanded that the Jews (among others) worship him as God-King. The normal Roman practice was to allow native populations full rights to carry out their own religious rules without offensive interruptions by the authorities. Josephus describes in graphic terms the passions aroused when Caligula broke this tradition:

> The insolence with which the emperor defied fortune surpassed all bounds: he wished to be considered a god and to be hailed as such. He cut off the flower of the nobility of his country, and his impiety extended even to Judaea. He sent Petronius with an army to Jerusalem to install in the sanctuary statues of himself; in the event of the Jews refusing to admit them, his orders were to put the recalcitrants to death and to reduce the whole nation to slavery.[17]

The outcry, Josephus says, was enormous. The Jews faced death without hesitation in refusing to have the images set up in the Temple and elsewhere in the country. When news of the crisis reached the large and powerful Jewish community in Egypt, a delegation to Rome and a letter of protest were organized, with the philosopher Philo taking part. The story is also absorbing in that, for once, it had a happy ending. Before Petronius could be punished by Caligula for his attempts to come to terms with the Jews, Caligula was assassinated (in 61 CE) and succeeded by the far more tolerant Claudius.

The Caligula story can be seen as a manifestation of the deeply ingrained rejection of paganism in all its forms – the worship of idols, the concept of kings as gods – going back in origin to the formative years of the Hebrew faith in Mesopotamia. As we have already seen, the fertility rituals of this background portrayed a struggle between many gods, magical in power though quasi-human in character. In the battles they fought, the outcome was always presented as a cliff-hanger. The mighty struggle with its happy ending often included a fight with a sea-monster, whose defeat allowed the chaos of the seas to be re-ordered into heaven and earth as at Creation.

It is just over a hundred years since a detailed picture of the Babylonian version of the Near Eastern myth emerged through the excavation at Nineveh of seven Tablets, written down at the beginning of the second millenium BCE and published, after decipherment, in 1876. If it was the essence of the nascent Hebrew faith to reject these myths, an awareness of their nature undoubtedly lingered in the Hebrew unconscious. In particular, as we shall see in the next chapter, imagery from these myths, in the Canaanite as well as the Babylonian forms, found expression from time to time in the archaic imagery of the Bible itself. But if echoes of this kind are now recognized through a close reading of the Bible text, the main force of the Hebrew tradition was to reject anything like a belief in the divine nature of a king or indeed of any human being.

Here, then, is the purpose behind the emphasis given by the rabbis to the *Rosh Hashanah* theme of God as King, echoed for ever in the happy form of '*avinu malkenu*'. With familiar words of this kind, the Jews knew where they stood, self-confident enough to be immune from any dilution of their faith through echoes in the Bible of alien traditions.

Yet to be aware of these influences today offers a new kind of historical insight. For those who wish to follow this trail, as set out briefly in the next chapter, much is on hand to throw light on poetic images in the Bible, with festival overtones, that benefit from this kind of illumination.

5

Widening the Bible Background

BATTLES OF THE GODS

It is easy for me to imagine with what distaste my father, a *chazan* (cantor), who knew the entire book of Psalms by heart, would have reacted to the information that some of the passages he recited so lovingly in his daily rota are framed in language that echoes some of the ancient myths of the *goyim* (non-Jews). He would have felt the same to be told that passages in the prophets, recited regularly in the *haphtarah* readings in the synagogue services, were related in terminology to this background. Why look for further meaning this way, he might have asked. As far as he was concerned, he was content with the Bible words as they stood, without trying to unravel their meaning through a new-fangled approach.

But maybe he would have enjoyed 'close-reading' the Bible text in this form as his son does, regarding it as a deepening of affection for the familiar words. Unexpected things do emerge, relevant for us to look at here because of their links with the festivals.

As already noted, the Babylonian myth, with its story of the struggle of many gods, has been documented for the Western world for little more than a century. What we also know is that this story of the annual battle of the gods was communicated to the pagan peoples at their New Year festival. It was a recitation they already knew, as with all primitive peoples; but they would be stirred during the recital into responses and hymns in forms they had grown up with. Their immediate guidance in the ceremonies would come from hordes of priests under the Chief Priest, or a king who was himself semi-divine in status through having been anointed. In all this there would be the high-points of sacrifice, with food consumed communally with the gods.

The picture is set out, as already mentioned, in the seven Tablets from Nineveh first published in 1876. The epic of Creation, prepared for the New Year festival of *Akitu*, was a liturgy or chant recited with magical incantations and known from its opening words as '*Emuna elish*' ('When on high . . .'). In the fourth Tablet of this story, the chief god Marduk is enthroned as king and arms himself for the battle with magic weapons: a bow and arrows, a mace, lightning, and a net holding the four winds in check. He kills the sea-monster Tiamat, splits her body in half and uses it to fix the sky containing the upper waters in such a way as to prevent the waters emerging. The story continues in the fifth Tablet with an ordering of the seasons, which includes, in an individual epic, the story of a great flood. This version centres on the adventures of a patriarch called Gilgamesh, who survives; but the story also brings out the idea of man's mortality, with the hero unable 'to cross the waters of death'.

The publication of the Babylonian Creation epic, with its story of a great flood, inevitably aroused enormous interest; but the picture of Near Eastern myth emerged for Jews with, in some respects, more vivid points of contact through excavations as recently as 1928, which brought to light the Canaanite version of Near Eastern fertility rituals. In that year, archaeological finds at Ras Shamra in north-west Syria began to reveal details of the life and literature of a city-state called Ugarit, which rose to power in the fourteenth century BCE and offered in its myth a galaxy of gods that included Baal, the arch-target of Bible denunciation. In many ways, and most particularly in language and imagery, the Ugarit stories proved fascinating for Bible studies, with the fragmentary texts that had survived easy to relate to Hebrew once the difficult decipherment of the cuneiform texts had been achieved.

The most intriguing element in the Canaanite myth is to see Baal (Hebrew: 'Lord'), god of fertility, portrayed as the hero of the story, in contrast to his role in the Bible as the symbol of pagan wickedness and deception. Son of El, father of the gods, Baal is 'rider of the clouds' and also, as Hadad, the god of thunder and lightning. His father tends to favour another son Yam-Nahar (Hebrew: 'sea-river'), against which favouritism Baal rebels, persuading the craftsman-god Kothar to fashion magic weapons for the fight against his brother. He is determined to resist the demands of the powerful Yam-Nahar (who stands for the chaos of floods and sea-monsters) that Baal be delivered to him. Baal is victorious in a direct battle with him. He is restrained by the mother of the gods, Ashtoreth, and his sister Anath from overdoing his victory, but in the course of the struggle he does slay the seven-headed sea-dragon Lotan (Hebrew: 'Leviathan'), a parallel to the slaying of Tiamat (Hebrew: 'depth') in the Babylonian myth. In another part of the story we learn of Baal's temporary death through an unsuccessful defiance of the god Mot (Hebrew: 'death'), which leads to a long period of drought and sterility on earth. However, Anath rescues his body after seven years, splits Mot's body with her sword and has Baal restored to life in triumphal ceremonies.

These are, of course, adventure stories, offering a very different kind of myth from the realistic historical stories that the Hebrews saw as the origin of their rituals. Yet the prayers for fertility are a parallel, and Ugarit's period of power in the fourteenth century BCE was close to Israel's renewed presence in Canaan after the Exodus. The linguistic overlap has proved absorbing to scholars, and it is of course interesting, too, that the Ugarit stories ascribe to their gods feats of power that also lingered in the Psalms. If one has been brought up on the Bible, the echoes are fascinating, as one discovers in a marvellous book by John B. Pritchard, which assembles all the discovered texts, old and new.[18]

At one level it is satisfying to linger on the parallels. In learning, for example, of the pagan myths about the battles of the gods to control the chaos of the floods, one reads with more understanding the imagery of Psalm 29, verse 3: 'The voice of the Lord is upon the waters: the God of glory thundereth: the Lord is upon many waters' and, even more explicitly, verse 10: 'The Lord sitteth upon the flood; yea, the Lord sitteth King for ever.' What has happened, of course, is that the ancient Hebrews de-mythologized the ideas that surrounded them. A battle between pagan gods set in Nature is translated into a concept of Nature under the control of one unitary Being.

In a similar way, an almost exact stylistic parallel in Psalm 92, verse 9, to a hymn in the Ugarit epic of Baal reaches a change at the end which establishes the highly significant difference. In the Baal epic we read:

Behold thine enemies, O Baal,
Behold thine enemies thou shalt crush,
Behold thou shalt crush thy foes.

The difference in Psalm 92 is that its climax reflects God's moral purpose: 'Behold thine enemies, O Lord, behold thine enemies shall perish; all the workers of iniquity shall be scattered.'

But if one is not surprised to find that close-reading of the Bible text opens up basic differences of belief, the general echoes are still felt immediately. When Baal defies the chaos caused by Yam-Nahar, it is almost in biblical style:

Lift up, O gods, your heads
From upon your knees,
And I'll answer the messenger of Yam,
The saying of the mighty Nahar.

In form, it is easy to think immediately of Psalm 24, verse 7: 'Lift up your heads, O ye gates; and be ye lift up, ye everlasting doors; and the King of glory shall come in.' Behind the content, it is the parallelism which is so characteristic. One has always been aware of this, of course, in any reading of the poetic passages of the Bible. The new confirmation in Ugarit literature that this was the dominant style in the surrounding pagan literature of the period of Israel's resettlement in the ancestral land has a significance far beyond a natural interest in analysing the Bible text.

The point in brief is that the material now available puts an end to views that were originally held by 'higher critics', mostly from Germany, that the monotheism ascribed to Moses could not have been put forward in his time, if he indeed existed. Monotheism and the supreme poetry of the Psalms and the prophets must have surfaced at a very 'late' time in Israel's history. The 'early' Hebrews, they argued, were too much part of their pagan background to have developed and expressed even in oral literature the revolutionary concept of a single God of all Creation. Today, this approach has been overwhelmingly amended. Scholars at home in the discoveries have been able to show from linguistic and stylistic parallels in the Bible with Ugarit epics and poetry that this is evidence of the authentic age of basic literature in the

Bible, expressed by a people who had already taken decisive steps to break out from the pagan world.

This new approach was expressed with great cogency by William Foxwell Albright, a famed American archaeologist who worked for years in Palestine and was one of the first to establish the true relationship of the ancient Hebrews to their background.

In his view, 'it was indeed Moses who was the principal architect of Israelite monotheism. Without monotheism, Israel as we know it would not have existed.' The background influence was, of course, very strong. One has to recognize 'much exchange of cultural influences between Israel and its neighbours on all sides of its tiny territory'. But though there were many irruptions of paganism, 'Israelite authors were able to utilize it without permitting it seriously to distort their monotheistic approach'.[19]

The ambivalence, or the razor's edge, is on display most clearly in Bible literature surviving from the early period of resettlement. It is, in effect, the underlying theme of the book of *Judges*, when 'everyone did what was right in his own eyes'. Each story, brilliantly graphic in detail, dramatizes the emergence of a transient leader, inspired by the ancient faith, who faces endless challenges from pagan-oriented Hebrews but holds his own. In the course of the story, we encounter the proliferation of idols of gold or silver as disturbing to the faith as the ancient Golden Calf which had so dismayed Moses. But as each story is told, the detail leaves echoes that were to survive in style and imagery to later generations, often with a latent puzzle now cleared up by the new discoveries.

One example can be followed in the account in *Judges* (8:24) of the great hero Gideon, who received 1,700 shekels of gold from the booty that his soldiers took from the defeated Midians, and from which he made a golden ephod which people began to worship. There is another story in *Judges* (17:5) of an ephod being made from a colossal amount of silver, obviously for worship too. The Bible reader is puzzled because the usual use of the word 'ephod', as it appears in chapter 28 of *Exodus*, indicates clothing, part of the vastly adorned and bejewelled vestment and breastplate worn by the High Priest when he confronted God in the sanctuary. It seems clear enough that the ephod as worn by the High Priest was distinct in function from the ephod as a separate cult object, unless, as has been suggested, the vestments of a sacred object or person generated some sort of worship in themselves.

More convincingly, the pagan literature of Ugarit is shown by Albright to give us at last the original meaning of ephod as a 'woman's garment', something like a sari, fastened on one shoulder, leaving one arm free.[20] What emerges from two Ugarit mentions is a striking metaphor in which the dropping of the ephod is a symbol of God's power to bring existence to an end. The passage illustrating this in the Baal epic is full of interest for other reasons too:

> When thou dost smite Lotan [Leviathan] the
> primordial serpent,
> When thou dost destroy the winding serpent,
> Shalyat of the seven heads,
> The heavens will wither
> And will sag like the fastening of thy ephod.

For Bible readers there is an immediate parallel to the language of Psalm 102, verses 25–6, but with the story turned into monotheism: '. . . and the heavens are the work of thy hands. They shall perish, but thou shalt endure: yea, all of them shall wax old like a garment; as a vesture shalt thou change them. . . .'

The identical metaphor, but carried forward this time with prophetic conviction, appears in *Isaiah* (51:6):

> Lift up your eyes to the heavens, and look upon the earth beneath: for the heavens shall vanish away like smoke, and the earth shall wax old like a garment . . . but my salvation shall be for ever, and my righteousness shall not be abolished.

In noting special links from the adjacent Ugarit culture that lay to hand for the Israelites, one has still to see the prime influence in echoes of the Assyrio-Babylonian culture, established over long stretches of time. It had been received at first-hand through direct contact, and at second-hand from the Canaanites, themselves recipients of the pervading culture flowing so persistently from Babylonia. The new Israelite settlers escaping from slavery in Egypt would undoubtedly have picked up much of this from joining in Canaan those members of their kin who had never gone into Egypt with 'the Joseph clan'. In the formative centuries of the new settlement, the original Hebrew faith would go through a testing period of strengthening before it emerged so distinctively in the days of Samuel and David, to be expressed finally with such carrying power in the words of the Psalms and the prophets.

It may be helpful in assessing the festival evidence we have from these two Bible sources to be aware in advance that reactions to the pagan background are framed in their pages in very different terms. With the Psalms, the echo comes, as we have noted, in language and imagery. With the prophets, one looks for and receives a forthright argumentative rejection. The cultural anthropologist Theodore H. Gaster pinpoints this very effectively in a book published in 1969 updating Frazer's famous work, *Folklore in the Old Testament*. In commenting, for example, on some verses from the prophet Hosea, he says that much of *Hosea* 'may be read as sustained satire on pagan seasonal festivals. Not only are there significant references to sowing, ploughing and reaping, but there seem also to be a number of sly allusions to standard seasonal rites and myths.'[21]

He gives as an instance the verse (5:6) in which Hosea says that Israel will go on seeking God but will not find him, since 'He hath withdrawn Himself from them'. The reference here, Gaster says, is to the ritual search for the vanished god of fertility. In the Canaanite *Book of Baal*, Baal's sister, the goddess Anath, says expressly that she will 'go in search' of the ousted lord of the rains. An equally pointed comment on the pagan festival myth is applied to a passage in the next chapter (6: 1–2) in which Hosea calls on his listeners to return to the Lord in order to be healed: '. . . He hath smitten, and He will bind us up. After two days will He revive us: in the third day He will raise us up, and we shall live in His sight.' The reference, Gaster says, is to the staging among pagans at festival time of a mock funeral, 'and subsequent resurrection of the spirit of fertility'. There are examples in many cultures: 'in Egypt, it was Osiris who was thus buried and revived; in Syria it was Adonis'.

If the language of the prophets could (in this interpretation) look outward in satire, it could also, of course, look to inward memories, with as much grace as the Psalms, for a message that might be particularly moving at a festival celebration. One thinks of the famed verses from *Jeremiah* (2:2) in which the prophet is asked to evoke the steadfastness that his people expressed in earlier times. 'Go and cry in the ears of Jerusalem,' God tells him; 'I remember thee, the kindness of thy youth, the love of thine espousals, when thou wentest after Me in the wilderness, in a land that was not sown.'

50

This passage is read in synagogue at the New Year festival, as also is another one from *Jeremiah* (31:15) that is equally touching: 'Thus saith the Lord; A voice was heard in Ramah, lamentation, and bitter weeping; Rachel weeping for her children refusing to be comforted . . . because they were not.'

To find these verses as festival readings brings home the marvellous ability of the prophets to reach back in their speech to the folk-memory of the Hebrew people. This point is made very tellingly by the 'myth and ritual' scholar S. H. Hooke, in a book which gives full weight to the deeply ingrained Hebrew ideas which came to the surface in prophetic oratory. In this book Hooke is at pains to rebut the view of some scholars that a distinctive spiritual outlook was only a late development in Israel's history. In agreement with Albright, he says firmly that the true religion of Israel did not depend on the formulation of the eighth-century prophets; it was the experience of Abraham and Moses that established a feeling of faith and obedience, the vital seed which became the source of religious feeling that could be expressed from early times in a verse like that of Psalm 51(10): 'Create in me a clean heart, O God; and renew a right spirit within me.'[22]

Having established this essential point, Hooke is prepared to admit that there was some assimilation with Canaanite religious practices as Israel passed from semi-nomad and pastoral life to the agricultural and urban civilization they found around them. On festival celebrations he goes further in seeing some links, 'too obvious to be overlooked', between the Babylonian New Year rituals, centring (as we saw) on the renewed kingship of Marduk, and the Hebrew Psalms, whose theme is God as King. Scholars now call these 'Enthronement Psalms'. They include dramatic accounts of God's power, and their recitation is seen as a form of 'sacred theatre', dramatizing God's power.

Examples come easily to mind. Among the most familiar would be Psalm 29, with its vivid picture, quoted earlier, of God as a power in Nature:

> The voice of the Lord is upon the waters, the God
> of glory thundereth, the Lord is upon many waters. . . .
> The voice of the Lord breaketh the cedars; yea, the Lord
> breaketh the cedars of Lebanon.
> He maketh them also to skip like a calf; Lebanon and

Sirion like a young unicorn. . . .
The Lord sitteth upon the flood; yea, the Lord sitteth
  King for ever.

Gaster, under the heading 'A Canaanite Psalm?', spells this out in terms of the pagan imagery we have summarized earlier.[23] In the Babylonian New Year festival, Marduk, having slain the sea-monster Tiamat, is acclaimed king of the divine hosts and installed in a specially constructed palace to the adoration of his subjects. In the Canaanite version, the monster slain is, of course, Yam-Nahar. 'The *Poem of Baal*', Gaster says, 'was in all probability the cult-myth of a seasonal festival, its main episodes corresponding to the main stages of the ritual.'

The same theme is, of course, repeated in Psalm 93, which acclaims God as King because of His mighty deeds. At the centre of His might is His victory over the waters:

> The floods have lifted up, O Lord, the floods
>   have lifted up their voice; the floods lift
>   up their waves.

> The Lord on high is mightier than the noise
>   of many waters, yea, than the mighty waves
>   of the sea.

It is in the light of these deeds, the Psalm tells us, that God 'is clothed with majesty' and His throne 'established of old'. As with Psalm 29, the echoes of the background are very explicit.

In these and many other Psalms, the Jewish celebrant feels his feet planted very firmly on the ancient Near Eastern soil. It is with a sense of wonder that one recognizes this as a reinforcement of what has come down so distinctively in Jewish tradition. We shall have this firmly in mind as we turn now to the individual festivals, each with its own flavour.

Part Two

EACH FESTIVAL
ITS FLAVOUR

6

The Year-Through Festivals: Sabbath and New Moon

In turning now to the major traditional festivals stretching through the year in a straight sequence from Passover to *Purim*, it may seem a diversion to precede this by considering first two repeated celebrations, the Sabbath and the new moon, that override the familiar sequence. But there are good reasons for starting this way. One clue lies in the Bible, which often refers to 'Sabbath and New Moon' in a joint phrase to indicate their special position in very ancient times as popular festivities. There is also a deeper significance. Looking into the ancient past out of which the Jewish faith began to emerge, one finds that linking these two festivities in one phrase offers an illuminating paradox on the nature of Jewish distinctiveness.

The paradox lies in the twofold character of Jewish origins, still potent as a recognizable force in Jewish experience. On the one hand, the patriarchal Hebrews, as an integral part of the ancient world of the Near East, found a new role in history by revolutionizing ideas that were common in that world. Yet in some cases they were forging an approach that had no visible relation to the world around them. These two facets of Jewish life are exemplified in the two celebrations we are now considering: the Sabbath and the new moon.

Moon-worship was dominant in the Mesopotamian world from which the patriarchs emerged, around 1800 BCE, with Abraham the key Bible figure. At that time and in succeeding centuries, moon-worship in Mesopotamia centred on a large pantheon of assorted gods whose images proliferated in the temples. In the revolution in religious thought attached in the Bible story to the patriarch Abraham, the role of the moon as a god gave way to its recognition as merely one feature of the Universe created and sustained by a single Power. In following through this change, the descendants of the patriarchs turned moon-worship into a very rational kind of festival, in which contemplation of the new moon became a beauteous ceremony of simple rejoicing, expressed, as always in Jewish life, with a quietly recited blessing.

This 'adaptation' is very different in character from the story of the emergence of the Sabbath. Here we find an entirely new concept, a holy celebration of a seventh day of rest, a day of social and religious happiness due in time to be adapted in various forms into the heritage of all mankind. Yet if these two celebrations were so markedly different in origin, they were merged over the centuries for the Jews themselves into a shared tapestry of rejoicing, with each occasion retaining its individuality in a vast overflow of history and legend.

BLESSING THE NEW MOON

Looking first at the greeting to the new moon, we soon recognize that its meaning went far beyond its expression as a direct contact with Nature. There was always excitement, of course, at seeing the first tiny sliver in the sky, inviting a lively recital of prayers and psalms. More powerfully, however, it was a constantly recurring link with the festivals. As the Jews have a lunar calendar, the close observance of the appearance of the new moon was essential for festival dating. The New Year itself began with the new moon of the seventh month, Tishri. Two other major festivals, Passover and Tabernacles, began with the full moon on the fifteenth day of their respective months.

To get the timing right for these and other important dates, there was a careful system (as we shall see) for getting the exact time of the new moon's appearance over Jerusalem recorded as the correct festival base and then communicated to Jewish communities living remote distances away. From early times there was an elaborate system of sacrifices to express the happiness of the occasion, followed by a festive meal after the rituals. The unbridled holiday spirit of these celebrations in ancient times often called forth denunciation by the prophets (eighth–

sixth centuries BCE), who wanted every sacrifice to be a positive expression of the Hebrew faith in one God. Instead, the prophets saw something more like the original moon-worship of pagan Mesopotamia, linked to the moon-god 'Sin' and his daughter 'Ashtaroth' (Astarte), who was worshipped as 'the Queen of Heaven'.

Myths die hard, and the Bible is full of graphic detail showing how the ancient Hebrews slipped readily from time to time into celebrations that bore the mark of the original pagan practices. When the prophet Jeremiah denounced image-worship as the cause of Jerusalem's destruction by the Babylonian invaders, he was told by the men he reprimanded that they would do what they liked – 'burn incense unto the queen of heaven and pour drink offerings unto her, as we have done, we, and our fathers, our kings, and our princes, in the cities of Judah, and in the streets of Jerusalem' (*Jeremiah* 44:17).

To the prophets, this was 'an abomination', a surrender (as we would now say) to the appeal of folk-myth, in disregard of the moral teachings that called for constant expression. They saw these teachings flowing from the vision of the patriarch Abraham of one God, Master of the Universe, whose worship was to take the form of obedience to a moral code, embodying for the individual a choice between right and wrong. Abraham had expressed this faith in the form of a Covenant between his clan and the single Power of the Universe.

History in this form had begun for the clan of Abraham when his father Terah moved from their ancestral home in Ur of the Chaldees (in Sumeria) to Haran in the north, from which base Abraham would make the decisive immigration into Canaan. But if this decision to move into a new world epitomized the break with paganism, the social background of patriarchal life still reflected the absorption with the moon that, as we now know from archaeology, dominated Mesopotamian life. In some parts of the ancient world, notably Egypt, primary worship was to the sun-god; that this primacy went to moon-worship in Mesopotamia became very clear when the culture of this land began to be reconstructed in marvellous detail following the opening up in 1848 of the long-buried treasures and archives of Nineveh, the ancient capital.

Many hitherto puzzling aspects of the Jewish tradition were illuminated in this process. A notable example is the way in which all festivals, including the Sabbath, start with moon-rise on the night before. The reason is an echo of the way the Babylonians and Assyrians assigned the respective roles of the two great luminaries, the sun and the moon. In Western thought, the sun is all-powerful, the source of light, heat and fertility; however, Mesopotamian cosmogony took a different view: the sun is certainly powerful, but it is always predictable and limited in range in comparison with the moon. The sun emerges from a gate in the sky at dawn and is locked up at night within these gates, with no further powers until dawn. In sharp contrast, the moon, with its accompanying hordes of stars, takes off at night for a free rule of the Universe. Its movements are varied, never appearing at the same time on successive nights or in the same part of the heavens. Its rule is full of dark mysteries, with spirits of the night possessing sinister powers that affect man's fate on earth. With these free-wheeling powers, the moon sets the pattern for everything. Its varied appearances divide time into months and weeks, setting patterns for festival worship that govern the whole year. Flowing from this, close study of the moon and stars offers a key to the public and private affairs of mankind, with everything that happens during the day being started off during the moon's reign. On this view, the complete day is therefore the twenty-four-hour stretch beginning at moon-rise, an approach clearly affirmed by the verse in *Genesis*: 'And the evening and morning were one day.'

This is just one item in the carry-forward into early Hebrew life of the myth-world that had centred on the moon in ancient Mesopotamia. We noted earlier the drink offerings by the men of Jerusalem to Sin's daughter, the all-powerful Ashtaroth, 'the Queen of Heaven'. We can note equally the prophet Ezekiel's dismay (8:14) at seeing the women of Jerusalem sitting at the gate of the Temple 'weeping for Tammuz', the dead god of fertility due ultimately to be brought back to life by Ashtaroth. Countless anecdotes of this kind in the Bible make it all the more astonishing that during the long centuries in which the monotheistic teachings as formulated by Moses were often in an amorphous state, the underlying power of these teachings held their own until they could be given lasting strength in the formalism of rabbinic teaching.

It is perhaps even more remarkable that Abraham could have broken away so decisively from worship of the moon-god Sin when one knows today, through archaeological discoveries, that the great temples to this moon-god were at Ur and Haran, the two ancestral homes of Abraham's clan. Moon-gods whose names were linked to Sin had many locations in Mesopotamia, and may well have been carried nearer to Palestine itself if one sees a specific link between the moon-god Sin and the place-names 'Sinai' and the adjacent 'Wilderness of Sin'.

Accepting the strength of these ancient links, it calls for a great effort of the imagination to see the primitive myth-world of Mesopotamia turning into the quiet celebrations of the new moon that became familiar in later Jewish rituals. In the days of the kings, the time of the new moon had been a popular, even wild, festival, as we know from references in the Bible. In rabbinic hands, the welcome to the new moon was signalled more quietly by the insertion of special blessings in the routine prayers for the day. What survived, however, with the same original excitement, was the link with Nature, the waiting in the open air for the first magic glimpse, the feeling this generated that this little sliver in the sky promised festivals to come, and a comradeship with Jews everywhere awaiting the good news.

ANNOUNCING THE NEW MOON

The enthusiasm for celebrating the arrival of the new moon is reflected strongly in details given in the *Mishnah*, already mentioned in Part One for the lively picture it gives of social practices in early times. The new moon rituals come out particularly in accounts of the experience of Rabbi Gamaliel, a leading member of the family whose leader, Rabbi Judah Ha-Nasi, edited the *Mishnah* towards the end of the second century CE.

One important interest of the *Mishnah* lay in the procedures to be followed in deciding whether the new moon had actually appeared. We are told that evidence had to be produced by two reliable witnesses before an official court. The description is graphic. 'There was a large courtyard in Jerusalem called Beth Yaazek where all the witnesses assembled, and there the Court examined them. And they prepared large meals for them that they might be encouraged to come.'[24] Normally the witnesses had to stay all day and be prepared for the most stringent cross-examination:

How do they examine the witnesses? The pair which comes first they examine first. The elder of the two is examined first: 'Tell us how thou sawest the moon, facing the sun or turned away from it? How high was it, to which side was it leaning, and how broad was it? . . .' Afterwards they bring in the second witness and examine him. If their words are found to agree, their evidence holds good.

To help those unskilled in observation, Rabbi Gamaliel 'had pictures of the shapes of the moon on a tablet and on the wall of his upper chamber'. Cross-examination went much further before it was agreed that the new moon had appeared and could therefore be blessed. The cry went up: 'It is hallowed! It is hallowed!'

In similar detail we learn how the news was broadcast. To reach the people of Jerusalem, beacons were kindled on the Mount of Olives. To send the news further the rabbis employed a carefully chosen band of messengers, though in earlier times they had used a system of beacons that covered many miles. The method for this is described in detail:

How did they kindle the flares? They used to take long cedar-wood sticks and rushes and oleaster-wood and flax-tow; and a man bound these up with a rope and went to the top of the hill and set light to them; and he waved them to and fro up and down until he could see his fellow doing the like on the top of the next hill. And so, too, on the top of the third hill.

We are asked to believe that in this way the news could be carried from Jerusalem to Babylon. Starting on the Mount of Olives,

they signalled to Sarteba, and from Sarteba to Agrippina, and from Agrippina to Hauran, and from Hauran to Beth Baltin. They did not go beyond Beth Baltin, but there the flare was waved to and fro and up and down until a man could see the whole Exile (Babylonia) before him like a sea of fire.

It should perhaps be mentioned that these vivid descriptions were already close to an anachronism when written down, since the rabbis were by this time producing a calendar by astronomic calculations, linking lunar observations (needed to date festivals correctly) to a regular tally of years based on the sun, with the lunar account then harmonized to the sun's by the intercalation of an additional month when needed. Calendar calculations became highly 'scientific'; but this in no way impeded the pleasure afforded by memories in the *Mishnah* of earlier practices, or the linked pleasure of embroidering talk of the moon with *midrashic* speculation.

One such puzzle, for example, was why the moon is smaller than the sun when, according to *Genesis*, they were created as equal 'luminaries'. On this topic, as in similar *midrashic* speculation, talk was never too serious: the object was to exercise the mind. A view advanced in this case was that equality had led to jealousy, leading God to make one of them definitely smaller. The moon was selected because it naughtily intruded into the sun's domain by becoming visible sometimes during the day. Some rabbis disagreed: this was unjust to the moon. God saw this, they said, and made up for His wrong decision by surrounding the moon with stars, like a king surrounded by court officials.[25]

If all this free-wheeling *midrashic* talk of the new moon is remote in style from the rather gentle blessings and prayers later formalized, the links with the Mesopotamian background are still visible and relevant. It is exactly the opposite with the new moon's companion festival, the Sabbath, whose origins are totally obscure.

THE MYSTERY OF THE SABBATH

In the first flush of excitement at finding Mesopotamian sources or parallels for Hebrew institutions, the Sabbath was seen by some scholars as linked in sound to the Babylonian word *sapattu*, the name for the fifteenth day of the month which, as the occasion of the full moon in a lunar calendar, was held to be an auspicious day for winning the favour of the gods. To derive Sabbath from *sapattu* was thought to throw light on the Bible's linking of the Sabbath and the new moon. On the 'seventh-day' aspect of the Sabbath, it was said that the Babylonians had a seven-day cycle of 'unlucky' days, which might (for obscure reasons) have attracted the *sapattu* name.

It is safe to say that this kind of derivation for the Sabbath has little persuasiveness today. One would need firmer evidence for a connection. It is more natural to see the Sabbath as wholly at home among the Hebrews themselves, as illustrated in a number of ancient incidents in the Bible fitting in clearly with the formal forbidding of work set out in the Fourth Commandment.

There is no problem of origin for those who take the Bible literally, with the seventh day, as described in *Genesis*, God's own day of rest after the labours of Creation. The Fourth Commandment spells out this link (*Exodus* 20:11) as a pattern that all must follow, as part of the direct message from God conveyed by Moses. The antiquity of the rest-day has, in fact, already been recorded (in advance of the receipt of the Ten Commandments) in the story of the miraculous provision in the wilderness of 'manna' (some kind of natural bread), which fed the Hebrews escaping from Egypt. The manna had to be collected daily before it 'melted' or went bad (*Exodus* 16:21). On the sixth day of the week, however, a double portion appeared, half of which remained fresh for the next day, which was suddenly announced as 'a day of rest' when the 'work' of collection was forbidden. We are told immediately that this was also a religious occasion: 'a holy Sabbath to the Lord'.

The religious aspect was all-important and was later given form in a vast compilation of Sabbath law in the Talmud. That this was present from the most ancient times is manifest repeatedly in the Bible. A striking example is the incident, reported in *Numbers* (15:32–36), of a man being found gathering wood on the Sabbath, for which he was taken to court and sentenced to death, a sentence carried out in the populist way by 'stoning'.

This echo in the Bible of a very early entrenchment of a Sabbath mystique is reinforced by its attachment, in one version of the Ten Commandments, to the other unique principle of Israel's existence, the eternal memory of the release from slavery in Egypt. The connection surfaces in the slightly different version of the Fourth Commandment that appears in *Deuteronomy* (5:14–15), in which Moses tells the people of Israel before his death why it is important that the servants of the household must also rest on the Sabbath. This, he says, is to remind the people of Israel that they were slaves in Egypt, which is why the Sabbath has to be kept.

Yet despite these flashes from the very ancient past, the Bible still seems to provide very little graphic detail about Sabbath observance until its importance begins to be emphasized following the return of the Jews in the fourth century BCE, under the leadership of Ezra and Nehemiah, from exile in Babylon. Before this, one gets the picture almost accidentally. One revealing instance of this kind emerges from the sarcasm of the prophet Amos (8:5), when he talks of businessmen being unable to continue swindling the poor because merchanting has had to stop for the new moon and the Sabbath: 'When will the new moon be gone, that we may sell corn? and the Sabbath, that we may set forth wheat, making the *ephah* [measure] small, and the shekel great, and falsifying the balances by deceit?'

An equally suggestive hint arises in II *Kings* (4:23), when the Shunamite woman runs to 'the man of God' (Elishah) after finding her son dead, and her husband says: 'Wherefore wilt thou go to him today? It is neither new moon, nor Sabbath.'

The implication in *Amos* that business actually stopped on the Sabbath may be misleading as a universal picture since we find the prophet Jeremiah complaining that markets within Jerusalem were supplied on the Sabbath. The prophet Ezekiel took this further by picking out Sabbath desecration as one of the sins for which Jerusalem had been doomed. The message was obviously taken to heart by the leaders of the Return. Nehemiah emphasized that the Sabbath was central to the observance of 'precepts, statutes and laws', which would restore Israel's religious strength, a faith he had brought with him from the Exile (*Nehemiah* 9:14).

FULL EVOLUTION OF THE SABBATH

From this point on, Sabbath observance began to grow into the major base on which the rabbis later built. Whatever the Sabbath's origins, it had clearly been strengthened during the Exile, like the institution of the synagogue, as a way of restoring the pride that had been linked earlier to the monarchy and the Temple. The picture emerges clearly in the historical works of Josephus and in the *Mishnah*. Before the time of the destruction of the Second Temple in 70 CE, the Sabbath sacrifices had been expanded, together with a wide-ranging exposition of Sabbath law, at the hands of the Pharisees. There is, of course, a graphic reflection of the Sabbath in New Testament stories of the life of Jesus.

In the centuries which followed, Sabbath observance was, without doubt, the most recognized prop of Jewish existence. This was partly because the social routine of its observance became so natural. It was prepared for with baths and good clothes, carried through with familiar activities starting in Friday Eve gatherings, and continued with synagogue attendance, substantial meals and a feeling of general happiness until the approaching dusk as the Sabbath waned signalled the end of the magic.

Yet though the social routine was compelling, the Sabbath offered satisfaction that lay beyond this. The most tangible – though indefinable – was the way it expressed the concept of holiness. By definition it was 'a day holy to the Lord', and this made itself felt in its Bible echoes – the Creation story, home (with its candles) like a miniature Temple, and the reading in synagogue from the Torah scroll, which reached a high point in *Bar-Mitzvah* and *Bat-Mitzvah* celebrations. Week by week, the Sabbath offered a religious fabric to Jewish life with a power that was uniquely its own.

This feeling was shared even by those whose first thought of the Sabbath could be negative – that it was a day on which all kinds of 'normal' things were forbidden. The prohibitions were certainly endless, with everything linked in some way to the absolute prohibition of work on this day. But if this could be wearisome to some, it had another side that offered a special kind of intellectual delight. Given that the general will was to fulfil the Commandment not to work, there was room within this for endless discussion on the forms that this prohibition might take.

The flavour of this talk emerges with immense finesse in the Tractate of the *Mishnah* devoted exclusively to the Sabbath. The opening section, for example, leads off by defining one concept of 'work' in terms of carrying something from inside to outside a house (and vice versa), linked to a Bible verse (*Exodus* 16:29) forbidding routine activity on the Sabbath. With the *Mishnah*'s usual graphic detail, the talk turns to the judgement that a tailor might have to make in deciding on how close he can come to the Sabbath deadline in 'going out' of the house with his needle, which he might have to carry back after the Sabbath had begun. There is a parallel discussion on a scribe 'carrying out' his pen.

A moment later the talk turns to a discussion of the materials of which the Sabbath lamp may be made, which is not only interesting in terms of socio-economic history but in its reflection of the niceties of talmudic argument, combining memories of personal discussions with the most high-flown interpretation of the ultimate source – the Bible text. On materials for the Sabbath lamp, we hear talk of cedar-fibre, uncarded flax or raw silk for the wick, with mention of pitch, wax and castor oil among many of the permitted fuels.

All this is a tiny reflection of the detail in which Sabbath observance was developed. One realizes that the theoretical concentration involved in the relevant passages of the Talmud was not only the forcing-house for centuries of the intellectual powers for which Jews became famous, but that it was from the beginning, as it still is, a form of discussion sustained throughout by what one might call a holy delight in pursuing legal argument wherever it led.

An important facet of this was that a very large part of the definition of activities forbidden as 'work' was based on the Bible passage which reported that work in building the Sanctuary in the Wilderness had to be suspended on the Sabbath. Going back to the marvellously detailed description of the Sanctuary in *Exodus* (chapters 35–40), the rabbis developed an elaborate system of 'basic' and 'derived' types of work which they called respectively *avot* (fathers) and *toldot* (descendants). This carefully structured argument not only carried great legal authority, but also had a strong underlying religious tone because of its derivation from talk of the Sanctuary in the Wilderness.

THE SABBATH IN LEGEND

Yet though this emphasis on the laws of the Sabbath was central to the concept of observance, it was accompanied – and perhaps overshadowed – by the Sabbath delight that took a less rigid form in legend and folklore.

Much of this grew around the happy celebrations of the Sabbath Eve. One legend had it that two ministering angels (one friendly, the other less so) always accompanied a man from synagogue on Sabbath Eve to his home, where the preparations were inspected – Sabbath lamp alight, table laid, the couch covered with a special spread – so that the 'good' angel could give it his blessing. The family joy was expressed in the father's blessing of his children and his recital of the famous passage in *Proverbs* (chapter 31) extolling the virtues of his wife as a true *eshet hayyil* (valiant, resourceful, tireless), 'whose worth is above rubies'.

Of all the myriad legends of the Sabbath, the most striking is surely that of the far-distant river *Sambatyon*, across which the Ten Tribes were led to captivity by the Assyrian king Shalmaneser after he had conquered the northern kingdom of Israel (722 BCE). According to the legend, this river – thought to be located in Media – was a persistent barrier to the return of 'the lost Ten Tribes'. The river's special quality, as indicated by its original name *Sabbatyon* (the Sabbath stream), was that it 'rested' on the Sabbath. During the week it flowed too fiercely to make any crossing possible. On the Sabbath, when it was still, a crossing was prohibited because travel beyond a certain distance on the Sabbath was forbidden by Sabbath law.

The longing among all Jews for a return to Zion fed this legend immeasurably. It grew during the Middle Ages with accounts given by many travellers and adventurers, who claimed to have authentic evidence of the river's existence and of the nature of the Jewish people settled beyond it, longing for their exile to be brought to an end. All the stories, and the quasi-messianic adventures that sometimes flowed from them, had a lively reference to the role of the river in ultimately allowing the lost tribes to return to the community of Israel. It is not far-fetched to see a contemporary resolution of this ancient legend in the immigration into the new State of Israel of many 'lost' Jews from the East, living until then in the distant stretches of land beyond the *Sambatyon*.

7

The Overall Festive Calendar

PESACH (PASSOVER)

Every festival, as we shall see, has an individual character that gives it its own validity, yet there is a sense in which, as a key to Jewish identity, Passover outweighs all the others. The deliverance from slavery in Egypt that is celebrated at Passover has always been more than an important moment in history; it is the fulcrum around which the Jewish people has always identified its independence and pride. If the jollity at Passover is matched in other festivals, nothing ever measures up to the historic sense of peoplehood that took shape, under the leadership of Moses, during the long, formative years of wandering in the Wilderness.

The matchless account of this in the Bible has always been rooted deep in Jewish consciousness. The symbol is the statement in the recital of the *Haggadah* at the *Seder* ceremony on Passover Eve that 'in every generation every Jew must feel as if he himself came out of Egypt'. It is a feeling that takes astonishingly realistic form, given that the momentous event it commemorates took place well over 3,000 years ago. The endurance of the feeling becomes understandable because virtually every statement on Jewish existence through these millennia has harked back to the Exodus.

The *Haggadah* itself brings this out by picking up for exposition the remarkable affirmation set out in four verses of *Deuteronomy* (26:5–8) in which pilgrims to Jerusalem declared their faith. The story, engraved for ever in Jewish consciousness, leads from the patriarchs to the experience of slavery, ending triumphantly with deliverance: 'And the

67

Lord brought us out of Egypt with a mighty hand and outstretched arm, with great terror, and with signs and wonders.'

This overwhelming rationale for the celebration of Passover has been strong enough throughout the millennia of Jewish history to harmonize all the otherwise divergent facets of the celebration. With bated breath Jews have relived 'in every generation' the dramas of the Bible story and recreated in the Passover ceremonies an exact echo of incidents and commands through which Moses finally engineered the breakthrough. At the heart of the Bible story was the roasting by every family of a lamb to be eaten entirely during the night. Blood from the lamb was to be smeared on the doorpost of every home to ward off 'the slaying of the first-born', the tenth plague on the Egyptians which proved decisive in persuading Pharaoh to let the Israelites go. We are told that because of the haste in which the escape was carried out, the bread for the meal was baked without yeast, taking the form of a 'biscuit' which has come down to us as *matzah*. In the *Seder* ceremony these are two of the three essentials to be highlighted: *pesach* (a bone to represent the lamb) and *matzah* (for the bread). The third is *maror* (bitter herb), to commemorate 'the hard bondage' that is also spelt out in the pilgrim's affirmation.

We have already seen in chapter 3 that each major festival marks an important stage in the agricultural year, with an additional rationale that links it to a major drama of Jewish history. Each of these elements enriches the other, with a happy outcome demonstrated in the rules for the festivals as laid down in the Bible.

For Passover, these rules ordain (*Leviticus* 23:5–6) that 'the Passover' itself is on the night of the fourteenth day – full moon – of the first month *Nisan*, with the festival starting on the fifteenth and lasting for seven days. The first and last of these days are full holidays with cessation from work, while the intervening days are *hol* (secular), a form of workaday festival days. Because Jews in the Diaspora could never be quite certain when the new moon had appeared in the sky over Palestine, despite all the efforts made to spread the news, the rabbis ordained that in the Diaspora the festival should last eight days, with the first two and last two 'holy', and the intervening days as workadays. This became ingrained in tradition even though the original motivation no longer applied after an astronomic calendar was devised and known everywhere.

Details of the original *Pesach* in the Bible parallel the spring sacrifice of all pastoral people as described by cultural anthropologists. In this picture, every family slaughtered a first-born lamb or he-goat on the eve of the full moon in the first spring month, an ancient tradition by which one warded off illness and plague in the year ahead. A bunch of hyssop was dipped in the blood, which was then daubed on the doorposts of the home, a ceremony which marked the participation of the god in the sacrifice. The food had to be consumed in the night 'in haste' (as in the Bible story), with anything left over burned to avoid putrescence. In a book on this subject by T. H. Gaster, 'bitter herbs' are said to have been added as a cathartic against impurity. The ban on all 'leaven' during the festival was an expression of the same warding-off of impurity.[26]

There was never a hard line between pastoral and agricultural people, which explains why the lamb sacrifice in spring is enlarged in the Bible story by an offering of grain, natural in spring by a grain-growing people. The ancient Hebrews were both. Passover therefore celebrates, in addition to its other roles, the beginning of the grain harvest, first of barley and then of wheat, the whole period lasting seven weeks from the full moon of Passover. In the Jewish practice, an *Omer* (sheaf) of the new barley was offered to the Temple every day after Passover to be 'waved' ceremonially by the priest. The *Omer* began to be counted daily from the second day of Passover for seven weeks, at which point the festival of *Shavuot* ('weeks') was celebrated. 'Counting the *Omer*' until the seven weeks were concluded became a recognizable stretch of Jewish life with its own traditions, as we shall see.

But if Passover pinpointed this lively celebration of commonly held folk traditions, it was overwhelmingly the festival of freedom, in a way unique to the Hebrew people. In the Bible story, this freedom for the Israelites to make their way through the Wilderness to a land promised to their ancestors would be a testing time of danger and hardship, crowned at an early stage by the receipt of the Torah at Mount Sinai. With superb drama, Moses, the agent of this Revelation, is not privileged to enter the Promised Land himself but only to see it from a mountainous peak nearby. It is there that he gives the people his farewell message – surviving as the book of *Deuteronomy* – after the forty years in which he had been their guide.

It is no wonder that this momentous story instigated a festival that exerted such a unique hold on the people of Israel once they had developed an independent life in their land, under their own kings. We noted earlier the extraordinary enthusiasm which generated a centralized celebration of Passover by King Hezekiah, rising to an even greater peak of excitement under a successor king, Josiah. With the First Temple destroyed in the sixth century BCE and in the Exile which followed, we must allow for a long period of indeterminate purpose in Jerusalem before a new sense of independence was developed under Hasmonean leadership, with ultimately a magnificently rebuilt Second Temple.

In populist terms, the founder of this revival was Judah Maccabee, first in a line of rulers who put an expanded Israel on the world stage; but if we are looking for the force within the Jewish people that was to restore the ancient festival of Passover as a crucial element in Israel's long-term sense of identity, the creative power lay elsewhere, among the passionately devoted students of the Torah – 'the Scribes and Pharisees'. Among many other developments, it was in their hands that the Passover we now know was quietly formulated, independently of the priestly dynasties whose power would turn to dust when war with the Roman overlords ended in the destruction of the Jewish state in 70 CE.

We know from the *Mishnah* that long before this happened, the rabbis – who gave Torah study a greatly expanded shape and logic – had generated the style of exposition that the Jews for all generations to come would learn to enjoy in the *Seder* ceremonies of Passover Eve. It is satisfying that the *Mishnah*, edited at the end of the second century CE, describes the celebrations of our current *Seder* in all its essentials.[27] Much of this ritual goes back centuries earlier to when the Second Temple still stood. A simple proof is that in discussing the rota of the four cups of wine at the *Seder*, the *Mishnah* quotes authorities and arguments from the time of the famous rabbis Hillel and Shamai, who taught before the Destruction. Going back even further, it has been suggested that passages in the *Haggadah*, which refer in a denigrating way to 'the Syrian Laban', reflect the period in which the Syrians were the overlords (second century BCE), attracting the opprobrium of the rabbis.

It is all the more remarkable to find the *Seder* going back in essentials to Temple times when the dominant celebrations consisted of public sacrifices in Jerusalem, in contrast to what developed later: a private family gathering in every house, with readings, prayers and songs. Yet the roots are clearly visible, so that we can say with assurance that our *Seder* ceremonies, with the four questions, the four cups of wine, the open invitation to all to participate and all the other familiar aspects of the *Seder*, are more than 2,000 years old. This is certainly an element in their continuing appeal.

The appeal lies also at a deeper human level, in the power that the most ancient of Passover prescriptions – the need to abolish 'leaven' from the household – has exercised in promoting among the Jewish people a sense of invigoration at springtime. In biblical terms, the abolition of 'leaven' was linked solely to *matzah*. In primitive times, this had led in 'renewal' sacrifices to rule out anything in the food forthcoming that might ferment and thus be impure. The rabbis developed a parallel formula for 'leaven'. In practice this meant an intensely strict separation of Passover dishes and food, resulting in a spring-cleaning – or invigoration – that was put in hand immediately after the feast of *Purim* one month earlier.

This is just one element in the joyous rhythm of life established by the Jewish festivals.

LAG BA'OMER (THIRTY-THIRD DAY OF THE *OMER*)

Lag Ba'Omer is a joyous one-day festival that is also a non-festival. It exists, in fact, as a break from the quasi-religious period between Passover and *Shavuot* to give people a day off!

The seven-week period from Passover to *Shavuot* had a ritual in which a sheaf of grain from the new harvest was offered to the priest every day. Every offering was counted off daily until the forty-ninth day, after which *Shavuot* was celebrated (see page 69).

This period of *s'firah* (counting) was endowed with a special character of 'restraint', similar in some ways to 'restraint periods' found in other religions, as an echo of ancient propitiation of the gods before harvest time. (Lent comes to mind as an example.)

In the Jewish version, the *s'firah* period rules out joyful occasions like marriage, or even minor pleasantries like hair-cutting. It is very common for periods of 'restraint' to allow for a one-day break, and this happens in the Jewish *s'firah*, when the thirty-third day of counting the

71

Omer is a holiday. It is called *Lag Ba'Omer* because in Hebrew the letters L and G stand numerically for thirty and three.

Even though the restraints of the *s'firah* do not make it a really sad time, the permit to drop all restraint on this day gave it a special flavour. For children especially it was always a day to look forward to. In the communities of Eastern Europe, school would be closed for the day, with the children free to wander in the woods with bows and arrows, and to play other games of their own devising.

There is a picture of this in the vivid childhood memories of *shtetl* life in Eastern Europe by the Jewish leader Shmarya Levin, drawn on later (see page 114). To him as a young boy, it was a day on which all inhibitions were relaxed, a festive break consisting mostly of youthful high spirits. With bows and arrows the favoured game, we have to consider the theory advanced by anthropologists that a spring holiday of this kind goes back in origin to a widespread folk-custom of adjourning to the woods on a set day to shoot arrows in all directions so as to drive out the witches hiding there and thus secure a fertile year. This, they say, was the origin of the Robin Hood legend in which Robin and his merrie men disported themselves in the woods around Nottingham. We are free to doubt whether this had anything to do with the origin of *Lag Ba'Omer*.

The Jews had, in fact, their own legends about the origin of the celebration. One was that it was the day, four and a half weeks after the Exodus, on which the *manna* first appeared in the Wilderness. Another tradition sees this day as the anniversary of the death in the second century CE of Rabbi Simeon ben Yohai, regarded as the founder of the mystical teachings that ultimately took form in the Kabbalah.

It is customary in the Near East for the anniversary of the death of an outstandingly righteous leader to be celebrated by a joyous pilgrimage to his grave. This has become customary in commemorating Simeon ben Yohai, whose grave in the village of Meron in Upper Galilee is a focal point for *Lag Ba'Omer* celebrations, with bonfires at night to round off a day of picnics.

SHAVUOT (FEAST OF WEEKS, PENTECOST)

When the seven weeks of *s'firah* restraint are finally over, the deeply

72

loved summer festival of *Shavuot* comes into view: a very brief but extraordinarily happy one.

It is presented in the Bible as a pilgrim festival without a date in monthly terms but simply as being held the day after the completion of the seven-week *Omer*, which takes the date (according to the rabbis) to the sixth of *Sivan*, the third month. Choosing a date was, in fact, supremely important to what has become a central theme of *Shavuot*: that it is the day on which the wanderers in the Wilderness received the Torah, following the descent of Moses from Mount Sinai. This great occasion is not given as the rationale for *Shavuot* in the Bible, which says only that the momentous Sinai day was in the third month after the Exodus. To assign this to the day in the third month which follows the end of 'Counting the *Omer*' seemed, to the rabbis, a satisfying identification.

What the Bible does select for emphasis is that this, the second of the three pilgrim festivals, was, above all, a harvest festival. Completing the cycle which had begun at Passover with the priestly 'waving' of a sheaf of the barley harvest, *Shavuot* signalled the closing stage of the harvesting of wheat, from which two loaves of bread were baked and presented to the Temple as a sacrifice. More broadly it was the *Chag Ha-Bikkurim*, the festival of first-ripe fruits of all kinds, a 'green' festival if ever there was one. There is a rhapsodic account in the *Mishnah*, quoted earlier on page 22, of the way the processions carrying the first-ripe fruits to Jerusalem were organized.

In a natural development from this, *Shavuot* became in time the festival at which the enjoyment of all kinds of summer foods gave intense delight, with a highly decorative background of plants and flowers at home, in the synagogue and in the country generally. The Bible allots only one day to *Shavuot*, but this was expanded to two in the Diaspora for the reasons of calendar 'certainty' mentioned earlier (page 68). The extra day was always welcome because of the many activities crammed into *Shavuot*, partly because of its unique association, even if not biblically authorized, with the giving of the Torah.

In firmly Orthodox communities, the celebration of this great event impelled congregants to stay up all night, filling their minds with readings that would express their sense of awe. On the eve of the first day they would return to the *beth-hammidrash* (study-synagogue) after the evening meal to read all night from a book called *tikkun*, a specially composed anthology containing fragments (the beginnings and the ends) of all the books of the Bible, together with similar illustrative fragments from the Talmud, the *Zohar* (a mystical book) and the *piyyut* (synagogue poetry). On the eve of the second day, they sat through the night again, reading this time the Psalms of David, who, as we shall see, has a special association with the festival.

Spanning *Shavuot* more generally, an extraordinary ode called *Akdamut*, describing rhapsodically the days of the Messiah, is studied and recited.

Akdamut was written in Aramaic by the *chazan* of Worms in the eleventh century. In a special sing-song tune devised for this poem, it presents a vision of the golden thrones on which the righteous in Paradise await the Messiah, under canopies of light which turn the whole into a vision of the stars. Their imagination has no bounds. They see the righteous as dancing arm-in-arm with God Himself. A mammoth spectacle is presented showing the legendary combat between the sea-monster Leviathan and Behemoth, the celestial ox which will be consumed at the great banquet of the Messiah. The text and a free-ranging commentary offer an awe-struck legend, which describes how these two gigantic monsters could overpower the whole world if the messianic force did not save it.

It is no accident that the arrival of the Messiah, 'son of David', is highlighted at this festival, since the book of *Ruth* is read, which ends by showing briefly that King David was descended from her. *Ruth* is among the five books of the Bible known as the *megillot* (scrolls), each of which is allotted a special time for reading: the *Song of Songs* after the *Seder* on Passover, *Lamentations* on the Fast of *Av*, *Ecclesiastes* during *Sukkot*, and *Esther* on *Purim*. Reading *Ruth* on *Shavuot* is enormously effective as a story set in harvest-time, which builds also on the unique appeal of Ruth as a character, expressing her loyalty in the famed words: 'whither thou goest, I will go'. That this Moabite girl identified with the Jewish people seemed a strong expression of the theme of the festival, the giving of the Torah on Sinai.

Ruth ends with a brief genealogical list purporting to show that the marriage of Ruth and Boaz led, over four generations, to the birth of David; and it is for David, tradition tells, that the Messiah will come, to be greeted in the rhapsodic manner described in *Akdamut*.

TISHA B'AV (NINTH OF *AV*: A TWENTY-FOUR-HOUR FAST)

A festival calendar which mirrors Jewish history has to accommodate its tragedies as well as its joys. It is no surprise, then, to find an immensely sad stretch of three weeks beginning little more than a month after *Shavuot*. The tragedy being commemorated is the destruction of Jerusalem and the First Temple by Nebuchadnezzar in 586 BCE, when a large section of the people of Israel was led into exile in Babylonia.

This *hurban* (destruction), expressed in a host of moving literary forms, burrowed itself into Jewish consciousness with immense power, conditioning an ethos which remained – one might say for all time – as a mainspring of Jewish feeling. The day on which it happened, *Tisha B'Av* (the ninth of *Av*), became a complete fast-day, the only one in the calendar to match *Yom Kippur* in length: from sunset to sunset. But a fast of more restricted length, from morning to sunset, was instituted ahead of this to commemorate the initial stage in the tragedy, when the Babylonian invaders broke into Jerusalem on the seventeenth day of the fourth month *Tammuz*. The three-week period between these two fasts became a time of restraint from many familiar joys – no weddings, no new clothes, no meat meals, and other limitations to normal living until the memory culminated in the great twenty-four-hour fast of *Tisha B'Av*.

The dark mood which enveloped the Jews increasingly during the three weeks was – and still is – expressed by the pious in rising at dawn to join the throng of 'mourners' in reciting endlessly long *kinot* (poetic laments). In observing the major fast itself, sorrow takes on an even more intense dimension. Often the final meal before the fast begins is very simple, centring on hard-boiled eggs sprinkled with ashes, as at a funeral. The synagogue is lit very dimly. The worshippers sit on low seats, their feet in slippers. The *kinot* flow on, but the central feature of the day is the unutterably moving recital of the book of *Lamentations*, in a sad chant used only when this book is read.

Lamentations, usually ascribed to the prophet Jeremiah, tells of the Destruction as seen by a survivor, in verses of immense simplicity and literary power. The effect can be felt in translation only if the rhythm is given the same terse quality. The first word in Hebrew, *Eikhah* ('How?'), catches the bleakness of the mood and is the title of the book in Hebrew. Continuing in the same spirit the opening verses, translated line by line, would sound like this:

> How lone she sits;
> The city big with people
>> Is widowed;
> Famed of nations,
> Queen of countries,
>> And now enslaved.
>
> Weeping, she weeps in the night,
>> Tears on her cheeks,
>> No comforter of all her lovers.
> All her friends betrayed her,
>> Became her enemies.
>
> Exiled is Judah in pain
>> And grievous servitude.
> She dwells among strangers,
>> Has found no rest.
> All her pursuers overtook her,
>> A narrow target.
>
> The roads of Zion mournful,
>> Bare of pilgrims,
>> Her gates desolate.
> Her priests sigh,
> Her maidens grieve,
>> And she – bitterness.

With equal emotion but also as straight history, *Lamentations* became the text, centuries later, for the historical memories of the rabbis after the destruction of the Second Temple. Taking each phrase of *Lamentations* individually, they read into it a pre-echo of the horrors they had themselves experienced, or knew of from participants, in the second *hurban*. The book collecting these memories is called the *Midrash on Lamentations*, and offers a very detailed, graphic picture of the period it describes. It is of special interest in complementing the history books of Josephus, while offering, at the same time, some valuable source material for classical historians.

But if *Tisha B'Av* represents a total absorption in tragedy, it, too, is transformed immediately afterwards by the alternating rhythm of Jewish history. There is a neat illustration of this in the prophetical readings prescribed for the Sabbath before *Tisha B'Av* and for the Sabbath that follows the fast.

The first of these Sabbaths is known as *Shabbat Hazon* ('the Sabbath of the Vision'), because the reading is from the first chapter of *Isaiah*, which begins with the words '*Hazon Yeshayahu ben Amoz*' ('The vision of Isaiah son of Amoz') and prophesies doom and destruction for the people of Israel because of their sinfulness. The Sabbath following the fast is called *Shabbat Nahmu* ('the Sabbath of Comfort'), since the reading opens with the famous words of the fortieth chapter of *Isaiah*: 'Comfort ye, comfort ye, my people.'

There is a parallel rebound from depression in other ways once *Tisha B'Av* is over. Among other things, there is a rush of weddings, held back by the restraint of the three weeks. If time allows for a ceremony on the Friday after the fast, the wedding festivities, spread over several days, find a happy ambience in the atmosphere of *Shabbat Nahmu*.

A more formal rebound is celebrated only six days after *Tisha B'Av* in a minor festival held on the fifteenth of *Av*. In origin this feast is a midsummer festival stretching back to early times, with no formalities and only pleasure the aim. It is paralleled in the Jewish calendar by a midwinter festival of a similar type on the fifteenth day of *Shvat*, the eleventh month.

In the autumn festival, there is a surviving rationale in it being regarded as the New Year for Trees (*Tu B'Shvat*, the letters T and U standing numerically for nine and six). Both these fifteenth-day festivals are ultimately nature days, which fit happily into the changing rhythm of the festive year.

ROSH HASHANAH (NEW YEAR)

With *Rosh Hashanah* and *Yom Kippur* (the New Year and the Day of Atonement) we come to a ten-day period of deep personal reflection and self-examination which is different in character and power from any other experience in the festive year.

We noted earlier in discussing the seasonal understructure (page 38) that in very ancient times the penitential exercises of these ten days may well have had a seasonal rationale as a propitiatory period, then universal, to ensure the success of the great harvest festival beginning five days later. In the Jewish calendar, the climax of penitence on *Yom Kippur*, the tenth day of the month *Tishri*, is followed by 'the festival of ingathering', *Sukkot*, beginning on the fifteenth. But though a preliminary penitential link would have great interest historically, it is overshadowed for Jews by the personal meaning that this period holds as a unique religious celebration, stretching back continuously in this spirit to the pages of the Bible.

The name of this ten-day period in Hebrew is *Yamim Noraim*, which translates perfectly into 'the Days of Awe'. As with the three-week mourning for the Destruction discussed earlier, the mood of the ten days of penitence is initiated ahead of time in very Orthodox communities before the period begins by synagogue gatherings starting before dawn for the recital of *piyyut*, in this case *selichot*, prayers for forgiveness.

Given the profound religious importance which has been attached to *Rosh Hashanah* for more than 2,000 years, it comes as a surprise to discover that the Bible is very vague about it. All it says is that the first day of the seventh month, *Tishri*, is to be 'a day of solemn rest, a memorial proclaimed with the blowing of horns, a holy convocation'. If one went by this evidence alone, one would see the 'convocation' as merely an expansion of the celebration of every new moon, on which trumpets were always blown. One might then see the special religious mood that now envelops *Rosh Hashanah* as a flow-back from the truly awesome celebration that the Bible does project for *Yom Kippur*, on the tenth of the month. But this would diminish the original meaning of *Rosh Hashanah* in a wholly unwarranted fashion. The many ways in which *Rosh Hashanah* has been observed since ancient times reflect the meaning it has always had in its own right.

We have to look first at a minor puzzle in that the Jewish year seems to have two beginnings: in spring with Passover (in 'the first month, *Nisan*'), and in autumn with *Rosh Hashanah* (in the seventh month, *Tishri*). The puzzle is resolved through history. In ancient Canaan, the Hebrews followed the pattern around them in which the New Year began in autumn after the end of the dry, infertile season. The calendar was different in Babylonia, where the battle for fertility was celebrated in the spring. The Jews adopted the Babylonian enumeration of the months, beginning with *Nisan*, but they still retained the older timing of New Year in the autumn. As we shall see, *Sukkot*, the great autumn harvest festival, is described in the Bible as coming 'at the end of the year'.

The autumn New Year also carried with it, from primitive times, an expression of renewal, a time when the world is reborn. Among pagan people, as we saw earlier on page 44, this took the form of a battle among the gods to defeat destructive gods in the year ahead. The Jews, abandoning the pagan battles, retained nevertheless the sense of complete renewal. *Rosh Hashanah* had become for them, with the world reborn, a day of moral assessment, by themselves and by God.

That this underlying feeling about New Year was dominant, despite the vagueness of the Bible itself, emerges clearly in the rich treatment of the festival in rabbinic writings, reflecting its exposition at least two centuries before the Destruction. In this setting it was decided that the *Akedah*, the Bible scene in which Abraham comes perilously close to sacrificing his son Isaac, was a drama so important to the emergence of Israel that it must have taken place on *Rosh Hashanah*. The passage in chapter 22 of *Genesis* describing the *Akedah* is, therefore, the Torah reading on this day.

In more personal terms, the rabbis built into *Rosh Hashanah* a dramatic presentation of how the individual's fate is determined by Providence in the year ahead. Symbolically, they imagined the individual's actions in the past year as having been recorded in 'a book of memory', out of which would flow an ultimate verdict for the future year: life or death. This verdict would be noted provisionally on *Rosh Hashanah*, to be finally decided and 'sealed' on *Yom Kippur*. There was room, then, for remission: 'Repentance, prayer and charity can avert the dread decree.'

This is a pervading theme throughout *Rosh Hashanah*, but as with other services during the Days of Awe, a moment comes in the synagogue ritual of *Rosh Hashanah* which expresses the underlying mood with particular intensity. The congregants await this moment with particular sensitivity, fully aware of its imminence and ready to respond.

In the synagogue service, the Ark of the Torah is opened, the congregants rise, and the *chazan*, with dramatic intensity, begins quietly to intone the awaited words: '*Unetaneh tokef...*' ('We will declare the greatness and holiness of this day . . .').

In its opening sentences, the prayer acknowledges the power of God, to Whom all is known. It is in this setting that the individual's fate is to be decided: 'Who is to live and who is to die, who by water and who by fire, who by the sword and who by hunger . . .' As the words move on, the congregants standing silent before the open Ark are drawn in awe towards a mystery that no one can solve. One is aware of fate, but also of the sense that it is within one's own power to affect fate by living a virtuous life.

The prayer comes to an end and the Ark is closed. With the spell broken, the service concludes with more traditional prayers and hymns. Solemnity gives way to greeting: 'May you be inscribed for a good year!'

The one-day gathering prescribed in the Bible was lengthened to two in the Diaspora as with other festivals (see page 68). On each day (except on the Sabbath) the service breaks off from regular passages at a set point to listen to the primeval call of the *shofar*. The notes are blown to a long-established pattern, with long, short and quavering blasts alternating to a libretto of instructions. It is an old world relived and sustained with strange power.

With the long service over, home beckons with a festive meal and New Year gifts in abundance. There is a jar of honey to symbolize the sweetness hoped for.

In the afternoon, an old custom known as *tashlich* (casting) calls for a promenade by an adjacent river, if one is available, so that one's sins can be cast into running water and flow out to sea. It is a happy, carefree ceremony, with all present wearing their New Year clothes. The greetings never cease: '*Le-shanah tovah!*' – 'A Good New Year!'

YOM KIPPUR (DAY OF ATONEMENT)

To fast for twenty-four hours from sunset to sunset is so dominating an experience that it might be expected to push all other aspects of *Yom Kippur* into shadow. In the event, however, this 'Day of Atonement', as founded in the Bible and developed later by the rabbis, is immensely varied and satisfying in the details that surround the fast itself. From the moment of the introductory ritual of *Kol Nidrei* on the eve of the day to the farewell of the *shofar* as night falls twenty-four hours later, it offers a richly endowed experience of history and faith that is totally engrossing for the participants.

One begins by asking what is intended by instituting a fast. It may come as a surprise to discover that the Bible itself never specifies a fast, saying only that on this day, the tenth of the month *Tishri*, 'ye shall afflict your souls'. Long before this general instruction was expounded in voluminous rabbinic writing as a rigorous fast, it must have developed in this form for many centuries and become deeply embedded in religious practice. It is with the rabbis, as recorded in the *Mishnah*, that the fast came to be related indissolubly to forgiveness for all the 'sins' of the year now ended.

An important caveat is called for on this. At no point in the Bible or in the rabbinic writings is it stated or suggested that the fast is a form of expiation and that strict adherence to it ensures forgiveness. Very much to the contrary, the fast dramatizes as nothing else could the action one has to take oneself if one seeks to be forgiven for past failures. Socially, one is called on to redress every offence in business and private life that falls below the high moral standard to be observed by every Jew. In prayer to God, one confesses every possible sin and promises repentance.

To take these steps within the setting of an immensely long fast celebrated publicly in common with fellow Jews promotes the corrective action called for with a force that is never likely to be reached in short episodes of private contemplation. The mystique of *Kippur*, with a variety of ceremonies that have been generated over the centuries, offers a theatre of collective emotion that has no parallel.

If one wonders why this emotional power should be released in a fast, scholars ask us to look back to the role of a fast in very primitive times when it was an expression of purification by the entire community before they could be worthy to share the sacrifice 'meal' with their god. Parallels to this are found widely in many cultures. In this view, *Yom Kippur* should be translated as 'A Day of Purgation' rather than 'A Day of Atonement'.

The sense of community participation certainly continued in many forms as we shall see, most notably in the mysterious episode of the scapegoat which was to carry away the sins of the community into the wilderness; but though this has immense historical interest, it can never lessen the individual's experience of *Yom Kippur* as a day of intense personal cross-examination. The memory that it recalls of archaic Temple ceremonies does speak to one's sense of history as a Jew; but one receives this as transmuted by the historic prayers and poetry that have moulded memory throughout Jewish history. In this form, the fast is dominantly the experience of an individual.

Kol Nidrei

We shall see in a moment that in Bible terms the central feature of *Yom Kippur* was the awesome entry of the High Priest into God's presence in the Holy of Holies. This has been magically recaptured in a ceremony that takes place in synagogue during the day's worship. But before this point is reached, the congregants will have participated on the eve of the fast in a gathering called *Kol Nidrei* ('All vows . . .'), which will always remain for many the most haunting evocation of the fast.

The name is taken from the opening words of a long statement – not a prayer – that precedes the formal beginning of the fast and sounds at first like a self-protecting renunciation of responsibility for vows or obligations unfulfilled in the year ahead. It is, of course, far more than this.

If it were merely a protective formula, it would be strange that it should have acquired the significance it has. It is certainly different from the usual instructions of rabbinic law and was, in fact, not known in the early rabbinic centuries, being first heard of among the sages of the Gaonic era, in the seventh to eleventh centuries. At one time, some scholars thought that the words might be a form of self-absolution for Jews who had been forced publicly to accept Christianity or Islam. This idea no longer holds the field, and some now see the formula as a reflection of the deepest purpose of *Yom Kippur* in social terms: a time in which one must put things right, repairing damage, forgiving hurt and thus accepting blame in advance for vows that might be unfulfilled by *force majeure*.[28]

This would not in itself have given the *Kol Nidrei* statement such abiding solemnity among Jews, and one therefore puts weight on other reasons, two in particular. The first is that the impact of the fast is so serious that a profound sense of awe governs the moment of its inception. Any statement made at this moment attracts the awe of the festival; and this will be particularly true if a moving – indeed theatrical – presentation has been devised.

This is precisely what happens in this case. The haunting nature of the recital lies not so much in its subject matter as in a plaintive tune in which the words are sung among Jews of European (Ashkenazi) origin. The tune – a slow lament in a minor key – seems to have appeared towards the end of the fifteenth century among Jews of Central Europe. Musical scholars see it as a folk-tune, drawn on later from the same general background by Beethoven and other composers.

In synagogues today, the appeal of the tune has come to be heightened by its theatrical presentation, with the *chazan* chanting it first slowly and softly, and subsequently repeating it twice with mounting tenorial bravado to its climax. During this, the Ark has been opened and the Torah scrolls carried with great solemnity to the dais to flank the *chazan* as he sings.

For all these reasons, *Kol Nidrei*, by far the most important evening assembly in the festive year, asserts and maintains its hold in a way that is all its own. With the inexpressibly sad notes floating in the air, the fast is now under way, promising an absorbing mystery of religious experience in the twenty-four hours that lie ahead.

The Temple Echoes

The central moment during the daytime services of *Yom Kippur* is the evocation, with great power, of the mood of a Temple ceremony that was unique in the whole year.

With the destruction of the Temple always vibrant in Jewish minds, the *Yom Kippur* ritual that had taken place there had immense appeal. The moment of truth, it might be said, was the entry of the High Priest on this day into the inner sanctum of the Temple, the Holy of Holies, to plead for forgiveness for the sins of his people. By highlighting this event during the synagogue service, a sense of identification is aroused, with the benediction of the High Priest brought vividly to life in the solemn mood of the synagogue.

An important aspect of the original entry of the High Priest into the inner sanctum was that for this purpose he assumed the most modest possible style. Whereas he normally left routine Temple duties to ordinary priests and appeared in public only in golden ceremonial robes, on *Yom Kippur* he carried out the entire service personally and prepared himself for the entry into the Holy of Holies by being robed simply in a white gown.

It was in carrying out the routine sacrifices himself that he prayed to God in a way never heard otherwise: by pronouncing God's name explicitly according to the letters in which it is written in the Bible. Hearing this Ineffable Name, the masses who had gathered in the Temple courtyard prostrated themselves in ecstasy, crying, 'Blessed be the Name and the Glory of His Kingdom for ever and ever.'

This first prayer and sacrifice centred on a plea for forgiveness of his own sins. After a long pause for purification, the prayer was repeated a second time, with the same pronunciation of God's name, in a plea for forgiveness for the priests. Finally it was repeated a third time, when he prayed for forgiveness for the entire people. It was for this that he entered the sanctum. The populace, now stunned into reverence, burst into fervour as they saw him emerge from an encounter which had carried with it a mysterious sense of danger.

'No Happier Day'

The recreation of this mood in the synagogue service is, it must be said, only one of the long succession of varied experiences that fill the day. All supplement, in one way or another, the basic forms of worship that appear at set times during ordinary days, but one is never in any doubt of the special underlying theme of sin and forgiveness. Sometimes this takes very intensive forms, as in the recital of endless lists of *mea culpas*, calling to mind the relentless pleas of John Donne's poem, *Batter My Heart*. At other times the theme is explored more gently in terms of a Bible story, most notably in the reading, during the afternoon, of the book of *Jonah*.

The original Temple background is never far from the minds of the congregants. The echoes are always strong except in the case of one archaic ritual described in the Bible: the dispatch of the scapegoat. The story as related in the Bible obviously goes back to dim antiquity. Two goats are set before the High Priest. One, chosen by lot, will be 'for God' and sacrificed as a sin offering; the other, identified as 'for Azazel', will be led into the wilderness, carrying with it symbolically the sins of the entire people. The goat will meet his death in falling over a cliff. No one

84

has determined what 'for Azazel' meant, but as described it must have been a primitive ritual of very great power. We are told that when the news of the scapegoat's death was brought back to Jerusalem, it released a great flood of relief.

And here, in this mobile picture of the primitive and the joyous, we get an insight into how *Yom Kippur* developed the way it did. Solemnity, however intense, would give way, when its meaning had been absorbed, to communal joy.

We have noted this more than once in discussing the festive year; and *Yom Kippur*, the most solemn of all the celebrations, is a prime example historically of this human process at work.

There is a passage in the *Mishnah* which talks of the particular happiness of two festivals, the fifteenth of *Av* and *Yom Kippur*.[29] We noted above (page 77) that the fifteenth of *Av* is a midsummer festival devoted to the enjoyment of Nature. It seems odd to find *Yom Kippur* listed with it so firmly; but the clue lies in the huge happiness that moved the people when the solemnities were completed. There had been a feeling of danger when the High Priest entered the Holy of Holies. The mood continued while the scapegoat was on his fateful journey; and suddenly, with the news of its ending, one could rejoice.

The *Mishnah* (as mentioned earlier on page 2) describes the joyous mood with engaging detail:

> Rabbi Simeon ben Gamaliel said: 'There were no happier days for Israel than the 15th of *Av* and the Day of Atonement, for on them the daughters of Jerusalem used to go forth in white raiments to dance in the vineyards. And what did they say? 'Young man, lift up thine eyes and see who thou wouldst choose for thyself.'

The *Mishnah* passage continues with Rabbi Simeon advising the young men not to concentrate solely on beauty. They should think also of family and the qualities of faith that will lead to true gladness. This is the gladness that will be crowned one day by the rebuilding of the Temple. 'May it be built speedily in our days,' he concludes. 'Amen!'

SUKKOT (TABERNACLES)

The festival of *Sukkot*, beginning five days after the great fast, has, like

Yom Kippur, a central theme that might seem to dominate everything but doesn't. With *Sukkot* it is, of course, the dwelling in tabernacles or booths; but this feature is, in a full sense, only one element in a multi-layered festival of extraordinary richness.

The real key to *Sukkot* is that it is, as described in the Bible, the major harvest festival of the year: *Chag He'asif*, 'the Feast of Ingathering'. In this it was so important as to be known quite simply as the *Chag*, the festival *par excellence*. Expressing this, it offered a number of days of continuous, almost wild, celebration in a variety of forms. But in religious terms it was at the same time linked closely to the period of penitence immediately before it. In this respect it developed a whole range of celebrations which extended the original seven-day festival and vastly deepened its impact.

The rejoicing and prayers came together in Bible times as part of the absorption with fertility. There are many references in the Bible which show that before Jerusalem became the unique centre of festival pilgrimage, the harvest rejoicing took place at local sanctuaries like Shiloh and Bethel that could be as orgiastic in style as those of the Canaanites themselves. Once Jerusalem was dominant, the formal grandeur of the Temple transformed the primitive style. We see this in action in the detailed accounts of *Sukkot* celebrations and dramas in the days of the Second Temple provided in the historical writings of Josephus and the absorbing descriptions, legal and anecdotal, which proliferate in the *Mishnah*.

Both these sources show how strongly the Bible's instructions on *Sukkot* observance remained the authoritative base. Dwelling in 'booths' – a natural convenience at harvest time – had been given specific Bible authority as a memorial to the temporary huts used during the forty years of 'wandering' after the Exodus. In this respect it was transposed into a symbol of the Exodus, the perennial element in Jewish identity. But side by side with this rationale, a fertility symbol of lasting power is defined in the passage (*Leviticus* 23:40) calling on celebrants to bring together four species of natural products for this purpose. These are 'the fruit of a goodly tree, leaves from the date palm, branches from a tree and willows from a stream'. If this began, as some think, as decorations for the *Sukkah* (as told in *Nehemiah* 8:15), they were transformed as time went on into elements of elaborate ceremony. The quiet rituals involved in displaying 'the four species' during *Sukkot* services grew into a mighty communal surge of *Hosannas* (Hebrew: *Hosha'anah*, 'Save us') on one of the festival days to express the prayer for rain in the growth period that lay ahead.

At the formal level, the original Bible instructions on 'the four species' came to mean that every Jew had to deploy, for the festival, a collection (owned or borrowed) of a palm and citron, together with sprigs of myrtle and willow, all to be 'shaken' and blessed at various points in the service. This became so entrenched that, as noted earlier, the rebel leader Bar Kokhba, holding off Roman attacks on his domains (132–5 CE), sent urgent letters to his commanders in the field ordering them to ensure that products for these rituals were dispatched to headquarters in time for *Sukkot*.

But it was in a special celebration at a formal level that this ritual was dominant. It became established (though no one knows when) that from the first day of *Sukkot* these 'bouquets' would be carried by worshippers in repeated circuits of the synagogue, at a certain point in the service, to the sound of repeated cries of *Hosha'anah* in a sustained prayer for rain. This ritual builds up in a crescendo of excitement to the seventh day of *Sukkot* on which there are seven circuits of the synagogue in this way. For this reason the day became known as *Hosha'anah Rabbah* – 'the great *Hosha'anah*'.

The intensity of the prayers on *Hosha'anah Rabbah* recaptured to some degree the religious fervour of *Yom Kippur*. This was even stronger when a special eighth day of *Sukkot* was added with the name: *Shemini Atzereth* (the Eighth Day of Convocation). By the eighth day, the gaiety of the basic festival – expressed in the *Sukkah* and palm 'bouquet' – had come to an end; and the added eighth day had a different atmosphere altogether, dramatizing for the last time the reverence instilled by the Days of Awe. For services on this day, the *chazan* wears the white *kittel* of *Yom Kippur*, intoning melodies that bring back the sadness of the penitential period, as if pleading finally for the purity of heart that had been the aim of the fast.

Yet joy is in the wings, to emerge with even greater power in the ceremony of *Simchat Torah* (Rejoicing of the Torah), celebrated widely as a ninth day to round off the festival, though in Israel and some other places the eighth and ninth days are merged.

Simchat Torah, when celebrated in the fully traditional way, intro-duces into the synagogue a joyous free-for-all that has no parallel. In form, the day marks the completion of the annual read-through of the Torah scroll (the Pentateuch), followed by the scroll being rewound in order to allow an immediate reading of its beginning. The spirit generated is both reverential and rollicking. Two selected congregants are honoured respectively as 'Bridegrooms' of the Torah at its end and recommencement. In the jollity which ensues, the worshippers dance around with the scroll in their hands. In Orthodox synagogues, women sitting normally in a separate gallery join the main throng. Drink is often served in this kind of setting – traditionally whisky with salt herring – to enhance the fun.

In Israel and the other places where the eighth and ninth days are merged, the joy is still unlimited; but though in this respect the spirit of the *Chag* is kept thoroughly alive, the original celebration of *Sukkot* included a great range of folk-ceremonies that are no longer echoed, except in prayer.

The theme of many prayers and hymns is still that of water, the source of all fertility; but without the Temple, the relevant folk-ceremonies have ended, one in particular. At some point while the Second Temple was still standing – perhaps in the third or second centuries BCE – the Pharisees had instituted a water ceremony which called for a libation of water on the altar, following the wine libation which was a daily ritual after the sacrifice of the day. The link is clearly with the very primitive ritual of pouring a little water on the ground or on an altar as a form of what is called 'sympathetic magic'; but when dramatized in the *Sukkot* ceremonies, it had become a much-loved celebration in its own right.

The water for the libation was drawn in a special procession from the Temple to the Spring of Shiloah. There, a priest filled a golden laver with the water for the ceremony. The populace, waiting at the Temple, grew angry if the ceremony was not performed according to the form on which they now insisted. When in one such ceremony the priest-king Alexander Yannai, disliking the Pharisees, poured the water contemptuously over his feet, the crowd of worshippers (as was noted earlier) pelted him with the citrons they were carrying for *Sukkot*.

But this libation was far outshadowed by another *Sukkot* folk-celebration which is also now lost: a dance by torchlight every evening in the Temple area called 'the Court of the Women'. This dance was described by participants as the ultimate in festivity. It was perhaps by mistake that the water theme came into the title of the celebration:

Simchat Beth Ha'Sho'evah – 'the Rejoicing of the Water-well'. The tradition, as described in the *Mishnah* and by Josephus, concentrates more on the massive illumination of the area by huge, golden, multi-branched *menorahs* (lamps). Torches carried by dancing men intensified the brilliance. Psalms were sung constantly as the dancing and torch-throwing went on through the night.

It is no wonder that the great *Chag* drew pilgrims to Jerusalem on a scale that outweighed all the other pilgrimages. All the dangers of the journey – vividly described by Josephus – were worth enduring for sights like these. Yet in the end, the abiding symbol of the festival remained the *Sukkah* itself, as happy a setting for festival joy today as it was in ancient times.

CHANUKAH (FEAST OF DEDICATION)

With the feast of *Chanukah*, as with *Sukkot*, an abiding symbol – in this case the eight-branched *menorah* – dominates the foreground, with a mass of accompanying history and folk-custom that gradually unfolds around it.

The *menorah* has become the festival's symbol because the traditional story of Chanukah's origin centres on the relighting of the holy lamp when the Temple was won back in 165 BCE after its desecration by the Syrian overlord Antiochus. The date of the rededication was the twenty-fifth day of the Hebrew month *Kislev*, which occurs in midwinter. The story as told in the Talmud says that the festival lasts for eight days because, by a miracle, a tiny vial of holy oil needed for the lamp kept it alight for eight days. The winning back of freedom joins the miracle of the lamp in the celebration of *Chanukah*. A *menorah* is lit in every home daily for eight days, starting with one candle on the first night and working up to eight on the last.

Around this traditional story, *Chanukah* has been celebrated over the centuries in both a religious and patriotic spirit. After the return of the Jews from exile in Babylonia, their land had fallen under Egyptian and then Syrian rule. The Syrian ruler in the middle of the second century BCE set out to make religious worship in Hellenistic style universal in his empire. As part of this he installed the worship of Greek gods in the Temple of Jerusalem, in flagrant disregard of the Jewish faith. A revolt, turning into a military struggle, was led by an aged priest Matathias, whose valiant son Judah Maccabee defeated the Syrians in battle. The first religious task of the victors was to cleanse the Temple from its desecration, with the lighting of the *menorah* as its crowning glory.

In these terms, *Chanukah* has been for 2,000 years a triumphant expression of the Jewish will to live in freedom. By the same token it became, as time went on, a festival of unbridled joy and fun. The underlying religious meaning comes through in the reciting of the *Hallel* psalms and other special blessings. The jollity takes the form of parties and present-giving, with card-playing smiled on as one form of pleasure, and with children particularly favoured by school holidays, money gifts and many traditional games. Like the Passover *Seder*, *Chanukah* has a special appeal because it comes alive at home, where the glowing candles and the singing of a very popular *Chanukah* hymn, *Ma'oz Tsur*, generates a particularly happy mood.

Was Omission Deliberate?

Nothing disturbs this mood when one looks more closely into the history of *Chanukah* and confronts some unexpected question marks. The first is that the story of the great rebellion was not included as a book of the official Hebrew Bible, and became familiar among Jews only through two 'Books of the Maccabees', one written in Greek, the other in Hebrew, which survived in translation by the Christians. They are included today in a miscellany known as the *Apocrypha* (hidden writings), usually printed in English as an Appendix to the Bible, a haphazard collection of writings rather than documents central to the survival of the Jewish people.

Perhaps even more surprisingly, there are only a few spare references to the festival in the *Mishnah*, which we have looked to repeatedly here for its graphic detail on the festivals. This is surprising because while 'official' history writing in Bible style had virtually disappeared among Jews after the Exile, the discussions of social and religious issues in the *Mishnah* and other writings was constantly expanding.

Chanukah was certainly celebrated in popular terms, as one sees from brief references here and there in the first century. A rough list from this period of joyous days on which fasting is prohibited (*Megillat Ta'anit*) includes it; and there is the mention in the New Testament (*John* 10:22) of Jesus being in Jerusalem at 'the feast of dedication, and it was winter'. One knows also of the engaging argument between the two famed first-century rabbis, Hillel and Shamai, on how to light the candles. Hillel thought that they should be lit in progression daily from one to eight, while Shamai thought the opposite. (As so often, it was Hillel's view which prevailed.)

Given the *Chanukah* detail that was certainly known when the *Mishnah* was edited at the end of the second century CE, one has to think of its omission as deliberate. The editing was carried out by Rabbi Judah Ha-Nasi, and it is generally held that he must have wanted to minimize talk of *Chanukah* because (as mentioned earlier on page 30) he had very good relations with the Roman authorities, the current rulers of Palestine, and was not keen to revive memories of rebellion against an earlier overlord.

In general, it must be said that the rabbis always tended to be pacifists. The central interest of life was to study the Torah, not to disturb the peace which made this possible. This is a point overlooked by almost all historians when they present the great Rabbi Akiba as giving his moral blessing to the courageous rebel Bar Kokhba, quoting an alleged remark that he must be the Messiah. Akiba could, in fact, never have believed that a leader as ruthless as Bar Kokhba was a kind of Messiah, despite a jovial remark relating to Bar Kokhba's unbelievable feats of strength.

The virtual omission of *Chanukah* from the *Mishnah* reflects not only pacifism but also the rabbis' general dislike of the Hasmonean dynasty of priest-kings who had established themselves, under Roman protection, in succession to the early Maccabee rulers. That the Maccabees became heroic to the world at large in later years – the subject of dramas and music of immense range – is largely due to the lively account of their story in the books of Josephus, whose presentations of Jewish history became immensely popular in the Middle Ages. Josephus was, in fact, the first to talk of the festival as 'a feast of lights', though without any reference to the story now traditional of the relighting of the Temple *menorah*. His account of the Temple's rededication puts the emphasis on the resumption of sacrifices, a triumph to be celebrated for eight days. In trying to explain the festival's name 'lights', he says, rather lamely: 'I suppose the reason was because this liberty appeared to us beyond our hopes, and that this was why the name "lights" was given to the festival.'[30]

A Link with Sukkot

There are other oddities which scholars have examined, including some links of *Chanukah* with the preceding *Sukkot* in the accounts of the Temple's rededication. One such (II *Maccabees* 1:18) tells the Jews of Egypt, to whom the account is addressed, that they can celebrate a Feast of Tabernacles at *Chanukah* time. Another (10:6–8) says that during the preceding *Sukkot* the Jews of Israel had been wandering in the mountains like beasts, unable to celebrate the festival. In consequence of this, it had now been decreed that *Chanukah* should offer 'eight days of gladness as in the Feast of *Sukkot*', to celebrate which they should bring palms and sing psalms. To some, this suggests that the eight days of *Chanukah* were a replacement for the 'lost' *Sukkot*. Another suggestion is that the formal rededication of the Temple was carried out in the seventh month (the *Sukkot* month) like that of Solomon's Temple (I *Kings* 8:2).

There is no mention in this that the eight days refers to the eight-day miracle of the *menorah*, or that the festival is known, as Josephus says, as 'lights'. Yet this name and the candles have a strong air of ancient origin, which has led some scholars to link this aspect of the festival to the widespread practice of a 'lights' festival in ancient times around the shortest day of the year. The *Sukkot* reference may suggest alternatively that if *Chanukah* was a 'postponed' *Sukkot* (with its palms and booths), it might have included the torch dancing of the *Sukkot* 'water-drawing' festivities mentioned above (page 88).

But if there may never be a complete answer to the origin of the 'lights' name, there is a perennial interest in noting the myriad forms in which the old instruction 'to publicize' the miracle was – and is – carried out. In some periods, caution dictated that a very public display of *Chanukah* lights should give way to keeping the candles burning only within the home, but fashions and security receive different emphasis at different times. In our own day, it has become common (partly under the influence of the Lubavich movement) to erect a huge public candelabrum for *Chanukah* in areas with a substantial Jewish population; but if this is effective in dramatic terms, it is not as charming or romantic as the scene in medieval Venice in which the *Chanukah* lights were carried around on the canals. The English scholar Israel Abrahams described this in his book on the festivals: 'The Jews would embark on gondolas and row through their district, greeting each illuminated house with a benediction and a merry Hebrew chorus.'[31] Presumably in the intervals of singing they had fun with the *Chanukah dreidel* (spinning top), and enjoyed the consumption of the Venetian equivalent of *Chanukah latkes* (potato cakes).

PURIM (THE FESTIVAL OF LOTS)

The Jewish festival calendar ends with *Purim*, a one-day carnival in *Adar*, the twelfth month. It is as joyous as *Chanukah* but in a very different style. Unlike *Chanukah*, it is based on a book of the Bible, *Esther*, which tells how this beautiful Jewish girl saves her people. Chosen as the wife of the Persian king, she is then able, with her uncle Mordecai, to foil the plot of the villainous Haman to have all the Jews assassinated on a day he has chosen 'by lot'. For further documentation, there is a whole tractate of the *Mishnah* devoted to it.

Despite this documented background, *Purim* is in practice a festival of joyous abandon. Unexpectedly this emerges in the most formal of settings, when *Esther* is read in synagogue on the eve of the festival. The book is read from its scroll, with reverential devotion, but at the same time with a continuous cacophony of interruptions, including laughter, jeering and applause. Everyone knows the story, but everyone is on tip-toe awaiting the next twist.

The celebrations outside the synagogue are equally familiar and joyous, but behind all this there is an abiding mystery. As a good read, the book of *Esther* is totally absorbing, but one still wants to know afterwards if one has to take it literally. This is in no way to question the reality in Jewish life of the star characters, Mordecai and Esther, or indeed of the villainous Haman over whom they ultimately triumph. As with any good novel, *Esther* is enjoyed at many levels. Most directly we share the excitement of the action, suffering with our heroes in danger, sighing with relief when all is well; but through all this we are also aware of the story as a paradigm of Jewish history for all time, with hatred of the Jews being generated for no reason, and with immense tragedies lying in wait as a result. In this sense, *Esther* is totally 'true' and is felt as such.

But this in a way impedes another kind of questioning. Where does the story come from? What is its real setting? What indeed is the meaning of the name *Purim*? On the Persian setting, the scholars are very sceptical of what is a key element in the story, that the king Ahasuerus (Xerxes) took a Jewish girl Esther as a consort. Another puzzle is that the names of our heroes are obviously drawn from the names of the Babylonian gods Marduk and Ishtar, though these names may also have spread to Persia. There is also doubt on the derivation of the name '*Purim*' from a word meaning 'lots'. It is explained in the book as recalling that Haman drew lots to determine on what day he should order his 'pogrom' to exterminate all the Jews, but this seems an unlikely origin. Much ingenuity has been expended in looking for a more likely derivation.

On this, the timing of the festival may be relevant. It is celebrated on the fourteenth (in some places the fifteenth) day of *Adar*, falling usually in mid-March, exactly a month before Passover. A suggestion by T. H. Gaster in his book on Old Testament folklore is that the name may come from an old Persian word *phur* meaning 'first', so that the name – a parallel to *primavera* – signalled the approach of spring. On the Babylonian location, he mentions that the carnival spirit of the festival may echo the triumph in Babylonia of their gods Marduk and Ishtar over their rival gods 'Hammam and Kisrisha' (Vashti in *Esther*).

Purim *as a Carnival*

Looking beyond these speculations, it is the linking of incidents in *Esther* to folk-patterns found widely at carnival time that suggests a background to this festival in the annual role-reversal – a brief moment of power by a slave or clown or some other version of 'the Lord of Misrule' – that is the key to the way the festival developed. Folklore offers many versions of a commoner appointed as temporary king between the end of one year and the beginning of the next, with a triumphant ride on horseback foreshadowing doom or execution, as happens to Haman in *Esther*. This was certainly all lived out with tremendous enthusiasm in the parodies and role-reversals that

94

burgeoned in Jewish carnival life on this day around the central characters of the festival story.

At one level, *Esther* is, of course, full of echoes of stories told in *A Thousand and One Nights*; but if the romantic elements of two separate themes – Vashti and Esther – are rather mixed up, the significance of the central Jewish theme emerges with masterly power. This is all the more remarkable since it is the one book of the Bible with no mention of God. What emerges instead is an untrammelled sense of the Jews as a people, owing total loyalty to their heritage, but without spelling out the constituent elements of their faith.

The only 'instruction' in the book is to celebrate a holiday on this day. Though all celebrations include the reading of the scroll of *Esther* in synagogue on *Purim* Eve and often on the next day too, the ancillary festivities, including many forms of rich *Purim* food, are very varied. In some communities, especially of Sephardim, the holiday spirit includes cessation from work and the closing of shops, but more generally it is the sense of theatre which receives the greatest expression.

Most obviously, the story of Esther is itself dramatized, either straight or in the hands of comic '*Purim* players'. There is certainly no shortage of scenes and characters, with court dramas, private rivalries and a great range of major and minor heroes and villains to draw on. But side by side with this, *Purim* became the occasion for an extraordinary display of intellectual wit, through a rollicking freedom to parody all authority on this one day. This even included parodies of Torah study, by the creation of mock Talmud passages of infinite subtlety. It was a process helped by a general permission to be free with the drink on this occasion. There was a hearty welcome for the saying of a third-century Babylonian teacher called Rava that on *Purim* one should drink wine until one does not know the difference between 'blessed be Mordecai and cursed be Haman'. In the original, 'until one doesn't know' is *ad-lo-yada*; and this phrase was adopted as the motto for the first *Purim* carnival held in the new town of Tel Aviv in 1912. Since that day, the hugely expanded carnivals of Tel Aviv and throughout Israel are known by this name.

A North African Purim

As a change from the voluminous accounts of *Purim* jollity that emerged from Eastern Europe, it is rewarding – but not surprising – to find the identical mood portrayed in a book about Jewish life in a small Sephardi community of North Africa. An artist called Rafael Uzan, who emerged from this background and now lives in Safed, has had his vivid childhood memories recorded by the writer Irene Awret in a book called *Days of Honey*, with *Purim* high in the list.[32]

Early in February, he recalls, the teacher asked the children to open their Bible to the first page of *Esther*. Word by word they struggled to decipher the Hebrew text, their hatred for Haman growing with every moment. Exactly a week before *Purim*, the teacher, his arms overflowing with rolls of coloured paper and a box of scissors, pushed open the door of the classroom with one elbow, to reveal the surprise:

> Playfully, our ordinarily caustic teacher held up the shiny sheets of paper, bright yellow, grass-green, blue, purple and scarlet, destined to be cut into the main characters of our Persian adventure. Older boys taught us the trick: fold, cut, unfold, and a paper miracle took place. Haman the scoundrel and his ten beturbaned sons stood up before me, each with one mean eye in the middle of his head, their little arms stretched heavenward to implore mercy.

From here on, the excitement mounted. Running through the village to carry his mother's cakes to innumerable aunts, the coins he got began to mount until he and his friends could bargain with Ahmed, the Arab horse-cart owner, for a pre-*Purim* drive through the streets. Still to come was the great moment on *Purim* itself when the children assembled in the school courtyard to set on fire with fiendish delight all the paper cages they had built to hold Haman and his family.

The pattern is universal, and with one additional factor that is relevant to the subject of this book as a whole. In every Jewish community, the delight of *Purim* was a marker that now they were free to begin work on the massive task of house-cleaning and other preparations for the feast of Passover, exactly one month ahead. Passover was the renewal of life after the travails of the year now over.

What Rafael remembered from the little village in Tunisia would apply everywhere: 'Passover preparations got under way the very moment *Purim* flickered out. There was so much to be done if we wanted to celebrate our feast of freedom properly.' If the money would stretch, the Arab house-painter would be hired 'to daub everything with sky-blue lime, the first step on the arduous road to a clean, kosher Passover'.

For us, too, the story of the individual festivals has now come full circle, with *Purim* leading us back once again to *Pesach*.

Part Three

THE FESTIVE MOOD

8

A Festival Roundabout

THE FIRST *SEDER*?

This will be a discursive chapter, letting us wander among some occasions of festival life throughout the centuries to see how they permeated everything. Even without being subjected to chronology, festival experience establishes a sense of unity in that all the varieties of time and place give way, as the festivals come round, to a pervasive sense of identity that has reached Jews in all these circumstances.

We shall approach this here in what is basically a brief anthology of memories in various forms – history and fiction – that evokes the sense of identity of festival time whether or not a festival is the dominant issue. We are helped, not hindered, through the variety. Whatever the passage describes, one is immediately at home. This is a reaction that comes to everyone in an individual way, but there is always something in the air for those who are prepared to listen.

To start with something that might seem bizarre, we reach back for an illustration to possibly the first *Seder* as celebrated, the rabbis thought, by the patriarch Abraham. Abraham? How can that be, when he lived, as we know, hundreds of years before the Exodus from Egypt? Yet the rabbis were not wrong in taking one particular Bible story as an illustration of what we mean by the timeless perspective of Jewish history.

In the story, beautifully told in the eighteenth chapter of *Genesis*, Abraham, sitting at the door of his tent 'in the heat of the day', lifts up his eyes 'and lo, three men are standing by him'. In reality (if that is the right word) they are angels. Abraham rises swiftly to his feet and invites the men to rest and share a meal. He runs to the herd and

101

fetches a young animal 'tender and good' to be roasted for the feast. To his wife Sara he gives a substantial quantity of flour so that she can 'bake cakes upon the hearth'.

Well, there it is: a fine roast for dinner and something like *matzah* to go with it; it must have been *Seder* night! The rabbis had a point even factually, because a festive meal of this kind in the spring was part of the folk-culture of this pastoral people long before the Exodus angle was inserted to give it a vastly reinforced meaning. But they were being more than factual, of course. To them, Jewish history was seamless. Not only did Abraham foreshadow the *Seder*, but a whole series of Bible dramas – Jericho, Gideon, Daniel, Esther and many more – can be said to have taken place at Passover if one is prepared to be imaginative. So 'true' was all this that it became the theme of one of the songs now sung at the *Seder*. In the Hebrew, the title of the song is '*Ve'amartem zevach pesach*' – 'Ye shall say it is the sacrifice of the Passover'. The song is written in a very jolly style, which I can convey best, perhaps, in a free-wheeling version I included in my *Pesach* book, *A Feast of History*:

> He saw three strangers standing by,
>> Passover Eve, Passover Eve,
> Fed them a lamb, and they did cry:
> 'We're Angels sent by God on high,'
>> For Passover Day in the morning.

> When Pharaoh cried: 'O woe is me!'
>> Passover Eve, Passover Eve,
> God passed our doors, so all could see
> His firm resolve to set us free
>> On Passover Day in the morning.

> The walls of Jericho fell down,
>> Passover Eve, Passover Eve,
> And Gideon received the crown
> Of victory over Midian's town
>> On Passover Day in the morning.

When Esther called us to a Fast,
  Passover Eve, Passover Eve,
The gallows stood there like a mast,
But Haman came to hang at last,
Deliverance as in the past
  On Passover Day in the morning.[33]

GETTING HOME FOR *YOMTOV*

In every book of memoirs on Jewish life, an abiding issue is getting home for *Yomtov* (the festivals). It is all the more exciting, of course, if some long journey is being described; and there is a prime example of this in the delightful memoirs of an enterprising lady known as Glückel of Hameln, who began writing her book in Yiddish in 1689, after some years as a widow.[34]

Glückel was born in Hamburg in 1646 and was married at fourteen to a goldsmith and gem-dealer called Jose Goldschmidt (his profession), who lived in Hameln, a small town near Hanover. Though without formal education beyond the *cheder* (Hebrew school), Glückel read a great deal and was obviously very bright, as her autobiography shows. Though the background in which she lived was solidly Jewish, there were many bridges to the non-Jewish world promoted by business. Perhaps surprisingly, there was often, also, an accessibility to local rulers in some circumstances, since the rulers and other prominent non-Jews looked to Jews for all kinds of assistance and were quite willing to let favours emerge from this in good times.

A central issue in Glückel's memoirs is a preoccupation with marrying off her large brood of children; and it is in her telling the story of the exciting marriage of her daughter Zipporah that we hear about the long journey they made as a family around 1680, spending the festivals in various places but with the hope of getting home at least for *Sukkot*.

Her husband's business, though still modest, had been prospering; and when Zipporah was nearly twelve, a prominent matchmaker of Amsterdam broached the idea of a match for her with the son of a very wealthy family bearing the name Cleve (where they lived) and also a wider family-name Gomperz.

103

Once the idea began to grow, the proceedings took on a dynastic air. Elias Cleve had moved temporarily to Amsterdam because of a war in progress. Glückel's husband promptly went on a visit there and arrived on post-day, 'when people read their letters on the Borse'. As the rumour of the marriage spread, many refused to believe it, 'since Elias Cleve was a very rich man, worth 100,000 or more reichstaler', while Glückel's husband was still young, 'with a houseful of little ones – God protect them'. But the deal was struck, 'with a dowry settled at 2,000 reichstaler in Dutch money', and the wedding fixed for eighteen months later in Cleve.

When the time of the wedding drew near, they set off 'with quite a handsome retinue', Glückel with a babe at her breast, their rabbi, a manservant and a maid. The journey to Amsterdam was by boat from Altona, 'and I cannot describe the jollity and merriment'.

But now the final stage was approaching:

> Fourteen days before the wedding, with drums and dancing, and a company of more than two *minyanim* [groups of ten], we travelled to Cleve and were received there with great honour. Elias Cleve's house was really like a king's palace, handsomely furnished in every way, like the mansion of a noble. We had no rest all day from the eminent and distinguished visitors who came to see the bride. In truth my daughter was really beautiful and had no equal.

The wedding was to be graced by high society. Prince Frederick, later to become King Frederick of Prussia, was staying with the Elector of Hanover, who let it be known that they wanted to be present. The excitements were endless. As they gathered under the *chuppah* (wedding canopy), it was discovered that the *ketubah* (wedding contract) had not yet been drawn up. But all was finally arranged, and with the ceremonies over, they were led into a great hall, 'with regal delicacies in the centre, and each guest served in order of rank'. All this was crowned for Glückel by the universal admiration shown to her son Mordecai, then five years old. He was considered to be the most beautiful child in the world: 'The courtiers nearly swallowed him for admiration especially the Prince, who held his hand the whole time.'

With the return now to be faced, danger arrived, including tremendous storms that tossed the boat in all directions and the dread possibility that they might not be able to find the right accommodation for *Rosh Hashanah*, which was imminent, and *Yom Kippur*, a few days later. At this point, the outlook was not too promising. Disembarking, more dead than alive, at a little town called Delfzyk 'on the day before the Fast preceding *Rosh Hashanah*', there was no inn or Jewish home to be found: 'the prospect of lying on the street all night, without food or drink, was none too cheering'. *Rosh Hashanah* was finally survived, but now there was no ship to get them to Hamburg by *Yom Kippur*. 'The sea', they were told, 'is full of pirate ships. They rob everything they can lay their hands on.' They had already paid the passage money, so this was lost; but at the last minute, Glückel's husband secured a cart to take them to Hamburg by land, and they arrived just in time for the pre-fast meal.

With *Yom Kippur* over, the final hurdle was still to be faced. They moved by whatever transport they could find, and on the day before *Sukkot* had got as far as a village, which, they were told, was only eight miles from Hanover, where her husband's father lived. A wagon was secured and off they went:

> After all our hardships and sufferings, our worries and our trials, it was with great joy that we reached Hanover. My father-in-law came out to meet us. We saw him before we reached the town, like an angel, like the prophet Elijah, a staff in his hand, his snow-white beard reaching to his girdle, and glowing red cheeks. If one wanted to paint a handsome old man, one could not paint anyone handsomer. Our pleasure at the sight of him and our enjoyment of the festival are indescribable.

A *SEDER* BRIDE FOR SOLOMON JACOB

We move now from the bourgeois comforts of life in Hanover to a festival story set in a *shtetl* of Eastern Europe, as told by the Nobel Prize winner, S. V. Agnon, in his delightful Pickwickian novel *The Bridal Canopy*.[35]

The story opens with a *yeshivah bochur* (Talmud student) called Solomon Jacob coming to terms with a miracle that has happened to him. He is twenty-four years old and has been obsessed for a long time with the fate that has afflicted him, in his view, quite undeservedly. He is a skilful talmudist, fully at home in Rashi and all the other commentaries, and with a warm appreciation of the poetry and romance of the Bible. He gets on well with his fellow-students both in jovial argument and in the pleasures of life – like a glass of brandy – that surface in their company. Yet with all these talents he has not managed to achieve what was so normal with the others.

What he had wanted from life was a bed, to be shared with a beloved. Instead, he has had to spend every night alone on a hard bench in the *beth-hammidrash*. 'How long? How long?' he would say to himself, in a voice (Agnon tells us) as sad as the tune of *Oh come my beloved to meet the bride* on the Sabbath before the great fast of *Tisha B'Av*:

> How long? Men younger than he were already married and had children, while he was still single. Was he not a suitable young man? Why had they merited to be wed while he, the time for the breaking of bachelorhood many years overdue, had not?

All through the night he would lie awake until the footsteps of those who Watch for the Dawn were heard in the courtyard, and he would rise, wash his hands and put away his pillow until the following night.

But now a miracle had happened. A Jewish tax-collector, who lived in the country not far away, had come to town with an offer. His daughter, it seemed, 'had set her eyes on a gentile', so her father was impelled to marry her off before the whole country talked scandalously about her. When he came to town on *Purim* to hear the book of *Esther* read, he met Solomon Jacob and found him suitable. They shook hands on it and entered into a match.

So now Solomon Jacob lay on his bench in a wholly different mood, for he was a bridegroom-to-be, with a bride who awaited him. For Passover he was invited to the house of his father-in-law-to-be, where they would treat him with honour, give him all kinds of dainties and, above all, prepare him a bed. So now he lay on his bench

> continually estimating the width of that bed and the number of cushions and pillows it contained, each one marked with the name of his betrothed. Lord of the Universe! In thy great mercies wrinkle up the days that come toward us, and speed Passover Eve.

On the Eve of Passover he rose early, put on a clean shirt, prayed at sunrise and took a tractate of the Talmud with him to demonstrate his skill to his father-in-law-to-be. The village was two hours' walk from the town. He thought he would take a short-cut he had heard of through the woods. He set off, but the hours began to pass and he knew that he was lost as well as hungry. Why hadn't he eaten before he left? If he had gone to the village, five or six of his friends would have joined him and treated him to a glass of brandy with cake. And now his corpse would be found one day in the wood, long after Passover. As he thought of it bitterly, he suddenly saw a fine house with a horse outside and knew that it was the house of his intended.

All was wonderful. Out came his father-in-law-to-be, greeting him with the greatest affection. As they stood there,

> his betrothed came out of the kitchen, and stood before him pink and pretty, her plaits in her right hand and a smile on her lips. Shifting her plaits to her left hand she greeted him; and as her plump hand gripped his a quiver passed through him so that his tongue shrivelled up and he lost his power of speech. He bowed his shoulders even more, bent his hand and gripped the back of the Talmud book he was carrying firmly with his fingers. Said his betrothed, put away your Bible and sit down; and she took it out of his hands gently and put it on the table.

In came his mother-in-law-to-be, in festival array, 'veiled and adorned like a dowager'. The house was bright with festival lights; the table was spread with *matzoth*, wine, meat and green parsley. Everything was perfect: 'Solomon Jacob read out of the same *Haggadah* as his betrothed, holding his breath so that she shouldn't feel his presence, while she, far from being frightened by him, was actually touching him.' With the service over and the parents snoozing, the two young ones sat together reading the *Song of Songs*, as is done on Passover Eve. Solomon Jacob gave her Rashi's explanation of the verse: 'Behold thou are beautiful, my love, thine eyes are like doves.'

As they read, there was a whistle outside, but the girl went on reading in a sweet and happy voice: 'Tis the voice of my love; behold he cometh.' They finished the book. She took him by the hand to his bedroom, 'a room scented with pillows and cushions'.

'Lie down in peace,' she said to him as she left.

From the pillows was wafted a pleasing and gentle coolness. Stripped of his clothes, he stood beside the bed. How many pillows there were, and how many sheets! The verses of the *Song of Songs* were still whispered by his lips: 'Behold thou are fair, my love, and our couch is likewise fresh. . . .' Copper bowls and dishes gleamed from the wall. He lifted his foot towards the bed.

He stood there happily for a while, but suddenly he heard the housewife weeping. He turned towards the window and saw her standing with arms outstretched, howling and wailing, while his father-in-law-to-be ran half-naked after a coach which was dashing off as though driven by furies: 'Suddenly the crack of a whip rent the air. His father-in-law-to-have-been came stumbling back, his hand over his cheek, crying: "There's no daughter, no daughter."'

She had fled with her gentile lover. Tears welling into Solomon Jacob's eyes stuck his upper and lower eye-lashes together: 'One scalding tear dropped onto his right leg, which was lifted to the edge of the bed.'

FESTIVAL SECRETS FROM SPAIN TO PERU

Without much doubt, the strangest form of festival celebration was the pattern of secret gatherings, on the wrong days and with the wrong rituals, that took place in the sixteenth century among the 'New Christians' of Spain and Portugal. These were Jews who had been led into conversion on a major scale in the wake of widespread 'pogroms' that had broken out in Spain in 1391. Among the Jews themselves, the term used to define these converted Jews was *anusim* – 'the forced ones'. Among non-Jews, they came to be known as Marranos, a term that was clearly intended to indicate dislike but has remained uncertain in origin. Discarding fanciful derivations, the consensus is that it may have come from a slang word meaning swine.

Until this 'forced' or 'induced' conversion, the Jews of Spain had been free on the whole to lead richly independent lives, proud of their religious traditions while at the same time playing distinctive and satisfying roles under Moslem or Christian rule in the various regions of Spain. They had been able to make a special contribution to the life of

108

the Peninsula by being equally at home in Moslem and Christian backgrounds, which allowed them to build economic and cultural bridges which were valuable to all. As the Christian 'Reconquest' grew, however, with Spain taking on a single religious character, the change brought with it a disturbing growth of anti-Jewish feeling, stirred up by some fanatically fierce Catholic leaders. The Jewish position had become more insecure in some regions, with the outbreak of direct attacks in 1391 on a large scale leading finally to a surge of conversions among some of the Jews living in these places.

However, the underlying attachment to their ancestral faith was so strong that many of the converts thought they could keep this up privately, while adopting Christianity in a formal way. To some extent this worked, as long as the continuing communities of 'real' Jews offered them some sort of private link. The Church suspected this and argued – very mistakenly – that if Spain could manage to get rid of all the unconverted Jews, the New Christians would give up all the secret 'Judaizing' that was going on. This was a main argument behind the expulsion of the Jews in 1492, but in practice it was only partially successful; for though the Marranos were in a sense 'lost' after 1492, many held on secretly to the fragments of Judaism that lay, often only half-understood, in the family background. It became a seed that was due to flower again in the future, once they managed to get away from the Catholic setting.

In the meantime, the Inquisition set out to uncover any traces of the old faith that they could find among the Marranos. The *auto-da-fé* executions spread from Spain and Portugal to every Catholic country of the world. Every *auto-da-fé* was staged as a great theatrical occasion, with the judgement assured in advance, and with the penalty for many to be burnt at the stake.

This is a bitter story, though episodes of Jewish courage, as documented in the Inquisition records, light up much of the social history of the Jews at this time. The canvas is very wide; for though the accusations were couched in formal religious terms, they undoubtedly swept up much deep-seated anti-Jewish feeling to feed the flames of hate. Perhaps the most bizarre example of this is the great *auto-da-fé* held in Lima, Peru, in 1639, at which the Christian arguments against the Marranos were merged with an accusation that a great international plot – *La Complicidad Grande* – had been mounted by the rich

Jews of Peru to overthrow the government and free the country from Spanish rule.

It is relevant to the theme of the present book to note that the extraordinary persistence of Jewish links among the Marranos during these centuries turns out, from evidence now available, to have been based on their determination to find ways of preserving some of the festivals: not *all* the festivals, and not in the proper way, but with echoes that could pass from one generation to another in ways that could often defy easy discovery.

This handing-on process could be difficult and dangerous, as the historian Cecil Roth pointed out in his book *The Marranos*: 'Children were frequently brought up as devout Catholics, being allowed by their parents to be introduced fortuitously into the secrets of their faith by outside influences.' This could not be at too young an age, in case they revealed too much by childish chatter; on the other hand, if left too late, their Catholicism might be too deeply entrenched. There is some evidence, he thinks, that the right moment might have been around thirteen, which, for a boy, would coincide with the normal *Bar-Mitzvah* age. He also records that such traditions as survived were often sustained particularly by Marrano women, who told their children the stories they had heard and did their best to keep some dietary traditions alive.[36]

Among those whose direct connections had faded, one primary link was respect for the sanctity of the Sabbath; and this, as it happened, was not too difficult to hold on to. Though the inquisitor would be on the alert to watch for subterfuge on this day, one could quietly not work, and food could be prepared the day before. The most persistent tradition among Marrano women was the kindling of candles on Sabbath Eve, but this apparently 'normal' practice still had to be guarded against suspicion. Learning that a candle could not be extinguished on the Sabbath, they would often light it in a cellar, or put it into a pitcher. A book on the operations of the Inquisition in South America reports identical practices.[37] The candles for the Sabbath and festivals were often placed under tables or concealed by a black-out curtain. We hear also of the maintenance by Marrano women of an old Jewish tradition that when bread was being baked, a piece of dough would be thrown into the fire, as symbolic of the sacrifices of the Jerusalem Temple. This would normally not arouse attention, though an Inquisition informant who was a former Jew – a sadly frequent occurrence – might spot the link and put in a report.

In the festival calendar itself, only two – Passover and *Yom Kippur* – were focussed on, while the others were temporarily unobserved. However, one problem which arose was observing the correct date. Without guidance from the Jews on a 'Jewish' date, they took the timing from the Bible, fixing Passover for the first full moon after 1 March, and *Yom Kippur* for the tenth day after the first full moon of September. The adaptations of ritual were carefully devised to try to be as accurate as possible.

Looking back to the Bible, they could manage to follow the instruction on a Passover meal which centred on eating a lamb cooked whole. In compliance with a tradition which survived until recently among some Sephardi Jews, the celebrants dressed up for the occasion, booted and with a staff in hand as if ready for a journey – the Exodus. To conceal the preparation of *matzah*, this would be baked a few days after the full moon and eaten at that time. With Passover so central to the Marrano calendar, the variety of other links had to be watched.

This was less so with *Yom Kippur*, even though this was the major day in the year for the Marranos. Adapting the name '*Kippur*', they called it '*Dia Pura*', the day of purity. Fasting could be concealed, especially if they chose to be out of town at that time. Less easy was their religious desire to spend the entire day in company with fellow-Marranos, repeating such prayers as they knew and keeping candles alight in the evening 'for the living and the dead'.

New Year, Tabernacles, Pentecost, *Chanukah* and the other festivals had faded away, except among those families who were learned in the traditions they safeguarded. One change, noted earlier, was that while the joyous feast of *Purim* had disappeared, a rigid Fast of Esther the day before was sometimes retained, as symbolic of a parallel they felt between their own uncertain position and that of the biblical Esther.

Even with the festival links weakened in these ways for most of the New Christian families, this was by no means a universal pattern, as we know from the history of individuals whose life and work took them abroad, with an opportunity then arising for a more open celebration. Sometimes this attachment to tradition had a tragic outcome, as with a famous Portuguese soldier and diplomat of New Christian origin called Manoel Fernandes Villareal. He was close to the royal house of

Braganza and had been rewarded by being appointed Portuguese Consul-General in Paris, where he became a friend of Cardinal Richelieu. Returning home to Portugal in 1650, he was denounced by a fanatical friar as a secret Jew who had been in the habit of going to Rouen for the *Seder*. What followed is not a pretty story. Having been examined by the Inquisition in usual style – including torture, no doubt – he ultimately revealed the names of fellow-Judaizers. It did not save him. 'As a member of the nobility,' Roth writes, 'he was spared the indignity of being burned at the stake, but on 1 December 1652, he was garrotted.'[38]

In sharp contrast there is the story of the famous Marrano banking family of Portugal headed in the sixteenth century by the remarkable Gracia Nasi, who travelled in royal style to the court of Queen Elizabeth and the Netherlands in her guise as 'Portuguese' (the Jewish link being rather taken for granted) until she finally reverted openly to Judaism in Italy, becoming thereafter, with her nephew (and son-in-law) Joseph Nasi, a powerful leader in Jewish life. In similar, if not so exotic, style, a great many Marrano families preserved their Jewish links in this way, before settling in the Old World or the New World. The freedom they then enjoyed as Jews had been saved by their ancestors in struggling against all odds to celebrate the festivals.

HAPPY IN JERUSALEM, 1630

It is very refreshing, after the ambivalence of festival celebration for so many Marranos, to read a letter from Jerusalem, not far-off from Marrano-time, which expresses with uninhibited warmth the delight of being free not only to go on *aliyah* to the ancestral land, but to play a rewarding role there after risking all in a dramatic journey from Central Europe.

The letter we shall draw on is from a certain Rabbi Isaiah Hurwitz of Prague. It is included in a vast and fascinating anthology, *Letters of Jews Through the Ages*, which throws a fresh light on Jewish history on almost every page.[39]

Rabbi Hurwitz was a distinguished scholar who decided to settle in the Land of Israel after his wife died in 1626. He wrote a number of vivid letters to his sons and daughters who had remained in Europe. In the letter drawn on here, the timing of his journey is, as usual, linked to the festivals.

112

A modern pilgrim who gets to Israel today by air in a few hours misses out on what was once part of the fulfilment: the long, hazardous journey working up ultimately to the great climax. One hears it very much in the rabbi's letter.

The sea journey with a party of fellow-pilgrims was long enough: they were at sea for twenty-two days before getting close to land. To begin with, he tells his family, it was a very safe journey without any misfortune, which even had a bonus: the captain had set aside a special cabin for the study of the Torah and the saying of prayers. It seemed at first that by good timing they were going to be able to seal their success by landing at Tripoli just in time to celebrate *Rosh Hashanah* there. However, it was to their very good fortune the plan had to be given up. 'The Lord performed a miracle' which prevented a landing. Had they disembarked, Hurwitz learnt later, they would have been taken captive with all their belongings, 'because there was a great war raging there'. Instead, the captain set off for another port in Syria. A pirate boat pursued them, but with the help of a strong favourable wind they were able to escape. Within a few days they landed, 'in time for *Yom Kippur*'.

The next festival was, of course, *Sukkot*, five days later. They managed to get to 'the great city of Aleppo' in time to celebrate it there, and the rabbi himself stayed on for three weeks, overwhelmed by 'the affection and friendship' shown by everybody, and the respect paid to him. He sat in synagogue there, he says, 'just as in Prague, in honour and glory', with all the people eager to listen to his teaching.

From Aleppo he went to Hamath, and thence to the great community of Damascus. There they invited him to stay and become their rabbi: 'Thou shalt be our prince and we shall follow thee in every respect.' He was flattered, but the pilgrimage to the Holy Land itself was still unfulfilled.

From Damascus, he says, he went with his party to Ur of the Chaldees, 'the place from which our father Abraham originated'. He describes it as a journey of four days, leaving us with a puzzle. As there was no identification of Ur at that time, though it was certainly in Mesopotamia, a journey of more than four days by any form of transport, one is led to imagine that he must have been given travel-talk based on local legends. He is happy to provide details given to him: 'From Ur two fountains flow with miraculous fishes, which look as if they carry golden rings in their mouths. Nobody is allowed to touch them. So it has been ordered by the Turk since ancient days to honour our father Abraham.' He has plenty of similar marvels to relate: 'In Damascus there is a chamber in a cave where the prophet Elijah hid himself, and where the ravens brought bread and meat to him. This chamber still exists. I myself have touched it.'

He was now drawing nearer to Jerusalem, the ultimate aim of his pilgrimage. En route there he arrived at Safed, itself a holy city. Overcome by the sight of its ruins, he threw himself to the ground and kissed the stones and the dust. The ruins, they told him, had survived from the days of the Destruction of the Temple, which saddened him greatly; but while he was there, a special envoy from Jerusalem came to wait on him, with a plea that he should agree to become head of the *Beth Din* (Jewish court) in Jerusalem at any salary he asked for. Rather cannily he said that he would not accept a salary for this but would expect instead to be provided with a good and comfortable lodging. He had heard in Safed that there was a considerable shortage of apartments in Jerusalem, due to the influx of many Ashkenazi immigrants.

This was agreed; and, on arriving finally in Jerusalem, he found it 'the glory of the whole earth'. In more practical terms, he describes it to his family as a place 'of peace and safety, good food and delicious wine, all much cheaper than Safed'. He strongly advises anyone contemplating a journey to the Holy Land to settle in Jerusalem. He gives this advice, he says, not because he lives there but because it is really a good place to live, where nothing is lacking: 'The city is enclosed and surrounded by a wall. It is as big as Lwow; but the most important point is that it is particularly holy and the gate of heaven.'

It is the letter of a happy man, rejoicing that through his teaching he will, he says, be fulfilling the words of the prophet that 'out of Zion shall go forth the Law'. It is safe to guess that he found Jerusalem a wonderful place in which to celebrate the festivals.

THE ODOUR OF CANDLES

The Jewish world of Eastern Europe, now annihilated for ever, was the home of teeming masses who were apparently dominated by backwardness and isolation but who, in fact, expressed a culture that included

114

within its scope brilliance and love, dynamism and hope. There is no way of measuring the enormous talent that found expression later in the world at large as a transmutation of the inner life of Eastern Europe; but if one cannot measure it as a whole, one can see the story exemplified in a remarkable gallery of individuals.

In the nature of the case, none of these highly diversified men and women can be 'typical', so in a search for festival themes one sets out to find one individual for illustration, looking in particular for one whose dominance later in Jewish life reflected with special charm what the Jewish world of Eastern Europe had stood for.

A man of this stamp was Shmarya Levin, who was born in 1867 in a hamlet called Svislovitz. One picks him not simply because he rose from being a child prodigy to major roles in Zionism, literature and politics, but because he endowed all this with a wit of corruscating brilliance. If his great friend the Zionist leader Chaim Weizmann grew despondent, time after time, in his struggles to establish the idea of a Jewish homeland, the one cure he could count on was Levin's unfailing wit. We turn to him now, with the same kind of assurance, to bring back to us a picture of what a boy with poetic insight remembered of festival time. He left us his memories in a book called *Forward from Exile*.[40]

Levin was very proud as a child that Svislovitz was on two rivers, the Beresina and the Svisla, which flowed into it. It meant that for the *tashlich* ceremony of *Rosh Hashanah*, when Jews cast their sins in a ritual gesture into running water (see page 80), one had a choice:

> If you liked, you could patronize the Beresina; and if you liked, you went to the Svisla, flung your transgressions into it and had them carried down to the far-off Dnieper, thence to the Black Sea, to be lost at last in the oceans which encircled the globe.

If one thinks of *shtetl* life as isolated, one learns from Levin that life in Svislovitz was cosmopolitan compared with the life of the Jews who lived for the whole year round as primitive backwoodsmen in remote non-Jewish settlements, except for the few days on which they emerged to meet other Jews on the *Yamim Noraim* (the Days of Awe). These strange men were known as *yishuvniks*:

> There is no word for *yishuvnik* in English, for the type is known only to us. Months might pass without their seeing the face of another Jew.

115

We did our best to make them feel at home, gave up to them our nicest rooms, and in the synagogue assigned to them the places of honour. We children received the children from the backwoods with all friendliness. Some of them were wild creatures, terrified by the vast crowds of Svislovitz. The elders took special pains with them; my father would take some of them on his knee, caress and comfort them, and we would teach them some of our games.

But behind this, we also get from him an echo of what the Days of Awe meant to a *shtetl* boy himself:

Rosh Hashanah would have been a jolly festival if it had not been drummed into us that the Day of Judgement was at hand. God sat enthroned in the midst of his cohorts of angels, and one after another the tremendous account books were laid before Him, with their debit and credit columns of bad and good deeds. God decided who should live out the next year and who should die, who among the living should be sick and who well; and the prayers went into such details that my soul trembled. Young as we were, our elders had already breathed into us the terrors of death. I was scarcely more than a baby when I lay awake the night of the New Year and implored God for mercy on my father and mother.

The really testing time was to come a few days later. On the eve of *Yom Kippur* his mother told him, after the great last meal, that he must seek out playmates with whom he had quarrelled and forgive or beg forgiveness. This was not easy; but *Yom Kippur* took on its real atmosphere the moment one entered synagogue:

The floor of the synagogue was thickly strewn with hay. On all the window-sills, as well as on special tables, were ranged the huge white wax candles – the soul lights – which were to burn for twenty-four hours in memory of the dead. The windows were kept closed for fear a candle might be blown out; and it was accounted a good omen when the candles burnt evenly right down to the socket, without spilling their wax over the sides. There was soon created that special atmosphere which belonged to *Yom Kippur*. The room became hot, and the mingled odours of the wax candles and hay became thicker and thicker.

Levin's festival memories were for the most part untinged with this kind of solemnity. There was the wild dancing of *Simchat Torah*, when women were allowed to come down from the gallery to join in the endless Torah circuits. There was the *cheder* holiday of *Lag Ba'Omer* in the spring, when they played all manner of bow-and-arrow and egg games. Above all there was *Purim*, a month before Passover, for which they wrote and acted in traditional and modern plays under the direction of a doughty woman producer, the widow Chernik. But there was always in his mind, from *Yom Kippur*, the odour of the candles.

'WHO SOW IN TEARS . . .'

There are festival echoes in all the diaries which have now emerged from the prison-ghettoes in which the Nazis locked up their victims before sending them to the death-camps. The stories in each diary are too inhuman for comment. Words simply fail, but one must never forget.

Let us look very briefly at two diaries from the Warsaw ghetto, one by Chaim Kaplan, from the early stage when the sudden 'imprisonment' was a foretelling of evil yet to come, and the other by Abraham Lewin, covering the time when transports had begun and horror knew no bounds.

Chaim Kaplan was a schoolmaster who began to keep a diary, written in Hebrew, when the Nazis invaded Poland on 1 September 1939 and began to establish the locked-up ghetto. The diary was found intact twenty years after the war on a farm outside Warsaw, preserved in a paraffin tin. It was translated by an American scholar and published in 1965 under the title *Scroll of Agony*.[41]

Rosh Hashanah was on 14 September in 1939. In Kaplan's entry written at 8 a.m. that morning we read:

It is difficult to write, but I consider it an obligation and am determined to fulfil it with my last ounce of energy. I will write a scroll of agony in order to remember the past in the future. For despite all the dangers, I still have hopes of coming out of this alive.

Yesterday was a day of horror and destruction. Between 3 and 7 o'clock on the eve of *Rosh Hashanah* there was an air raid on the North Quarter which is predominantly Jewish. . . .

117

On the second day of the festival, the entry begins:

> Everything bears the stamp of war. Instead of Jews wearing *talesim* [prayer shawls] and carrying prayer-books rushing to the synagogue, one sees stretcher-bearers carrying the dead and wounded. . . . Inwardly everyone is preparing himself for death.

A year later, *Rosh Hashanah* was on 3 October. The entry for the eve before begins:

> There is darkness in our synagogues, silence and desolation within, and sorrow looking on from without. . . . Everything is forbidden. . . . Secret *minyanim* [prayer groups] by the hundreds throughout Warsaw organize services. . . . They pick up some inside rooms where windows look out onto the courtyard and pour out their supplications before the God of Israel in whispers. . . .

Kaplan was sixty at the time. He and his wife are believed to have been put to death in Treblinka either in December 1942 or in January 1943.

Abraham Lewin was also a schoolmaster. At forty-seven, he and his wife and family had been locked up in the part of Warsaw which the Nazis had finally enclosed as a ghetto in November 1940. There were more than 400,000 Jews sealed off in this way, but incredibly life went on: hungry and desperate as the Jews were, education, meetings, discussions, and even plays and concerts were organized, until finally transports to the death-camps dominated everything and life withered away.

Before this took over completely, some Jews had met secretly every Sabbath at dusk to exchange news and rumours. Lewin had been keeping a diary to present at this *Oneg Shabbath* meeting (a name which in happier times had meant 'Sabbath Delight'). Fragments of this diary were found after the war hidden in a milk churn and subsequently published in 1988 under the title *A Cup of Tears*.[42] The fragments which survived cover the period from 29 March 1942 to 16 January 1943, a crucial time following the final decision to murder the Jews on a mass scale taken at the Wannsee Conference near Berlin in January 1942. This plan was soon in operation and increasingly known to the Jews under Nazi domination.

The detail of the diary is horrific: 'When we look at the swollen, half-naked bodies of Jews lying in the streets, we feel as if we found ourselves at some sub-human level.' Much space is occupied also in reporting announcements and rumours, side by side with thoughts of what it could all mean to future generations:

> Those who are far away cannot imagine our bitter situation. They will not understand and will not believe that day after day thousands of men, women and children, innocent of any crime, were taken to their death. Almighty God! Why did this happen? And why is the whole world deaf to our screams? Earth do not cover our blood! Let no place be free from our cries!

This entry was written on *Yom Kippur*, 21 September 1942. By this time, we do not hear of festival observances, though we know from other sources that some Jews fasted and observed such rituals as they could. The festivals remain as natural dates for the diary, but often with the saddest of thoughts. An entry for *Rosh Hashanah* Eve 1942 is equally illustrative of gruesome practicalities and horrors, together with thoughts of how the experience has eaten away the moral substance of life:

> The people are quarrelling with each other. Anyone who has anything left cooks and eats and watches over their property. People steal everything they can lay their hands on, especially food. There is no feeling of common fate, of mutual aid. People wander around aimlessly like shadows.

The last entry in the diary is for 15 January 1943. A new *Aktion* (systematic transport) began at that time, and we must assume (says the editor of the diary) that Lewin perished in it. He thus 'did not live to witness the development of the Jewish Fighting Organization, and its herioc resistance to the Nazis first in January and then in April–May 1943'.

The diary is Lewin's memorial, fulfilling what he wrote in his entry for 6 June 1942: 'We want our sufferings, these "birth-pangs of the Messiah", to be impressed upon the memories of future generations and on the memory of the whole world.'

The Festive Mood

'. . . SHALL REAP IN JOY'

As if to blot out for ever the grim memories of festival days spent by Jews as victims of Nazi brutality, it was a festival day, the Feast of *Shavuot*, celebrated in Jerusalem on 14 June 1967, that marked one of the most triumphant celebrations of Jewish life. This day was a week after Jerusalem had been reunited as one city at the climax of the Six Day War of 1967, to become the capital of a Jewish state for the first time since its destruction by the Romans nearly 2,000 years before.

Until Jerusalem was reunited on Wednesday 7 June, the Old City of Jerusalem had been ruled by Jordan, who had quite illegally barred the entry of all Jews. This bizarre and distressing situation had arisen as a feature of the armistice which had ended Israel's War of Independence in 1948. In every other respect, this war had left Israel free to go forward as an independent state. This outcome had seemed most unlikely when Israel had proclaimed its independence as a state on 14 May 1948. The Arab states, who had refused to accept the United Nations proposal in November 1947 that Palestine should be partitioned into a Jewish and an Arab state, had intensified the attacks they had already launched on Israel from all directions. Against overwhelming odds, Israel had held on, but without being able to dislodge the very well-equipped Jordanian army from the Old City. The armistice negotiated at Rhodes in January 1949 had been based on current positions, with Jerusalem still in Arab hands. And now, nineteen years later, the miraculous victory of Israel in the Six Day War had broken through the final barrier.

Teddy Kollek, the valiant Mayor of Jerusalem, tells in his book *For Jerusalem* how the great *Shavuot* celebration took place. Some time earlier, when the usual preparations were being made for celebrating the anniversary of the May 1948 Declaration of Independence, a decision was taken to stage the parade in Jerusalem this time: in the 'new' part, of course. The secular date of the Declaration, 14 May, would coincide with the Hebrew date for the first time since 1948. With this in mind and Jerusalem the venue, Kollek secured support for his idea that they should commission a special song about Jerusalem, *Jerusalem the Gold*, which was sung for the first time on 15 May and, as he says, 'became the hymn of the Six Day War'.[43]

For months before this, the Government of Israel had become

120

extremely apprehensive over the fact that the Arab states, quite openly, had begun massing for a new attack on Israel. The UN force had been turned out of Sinai by Egypt, and President Nasser was also blockading the Gulf of Akaba. Egypt and Jordan had forged a new alliance against Israel, and troops in support began pouring in from Algeria, Morocco, Kuwait and Saudi Arabia. The slogan that Israel was to be pushed into the sea was heard non-stop on the Arab radio. Every Jew in the world trembled for Israel. Determined not to be a sitting duck, Israel itself mounted a pre-emptive attack on Egypt on Monday morning, 5 June. In one strike, it annihilated the Egyptian air force. On the next day, Israel girded itself against a new attack by Jordan; and, on Wednesday 7 June, Israel's troops captured Jerusalem and opened the way through the Old City to the Western Wall.

Without waiting for a cease-fire, thousands of Jews began pouring into the Old City to get to the Wall. The Feast of *Shavuot* was only a few days ahead. It was certain that hundreds of thousands would make this the focus of a new kind of pilgrimage. As Kollek puts it: 'The pent-up feelings of a generation would express themselves in the chance to touch the stones of the Wall once more, to pray at the holiest of Holy Places.'[44] As things stood, it would be impossible for the pilgrims to get through the narrow streets in these numbers. It was therefore decided to demolish some hovels that blocked the way; and in time for *Shavuot* the great Plaza that now stands before the Wall had been made ready.

It was a moment never forgotten by any who were alive at this time. For Kollek, 'the unification of Jerusalem was the most exciting period of my life'. In Jewish tradition, *Shavuot* celebrated the Giving of the Torah at Sinai; now a new significance had been added.

MY MOTHER DIED ON *SHAVUOT*
Yehuda Amichai

My mother died on *Shavuot* when they finished counting the
    Omer,
her oldest brother died in 1916, fallen in the war,
I almost fell in 1948,
and my mother died in 1983.
Everyone dies at some counting,
long or short,
everyone falls in a war,
they all deserve a wreath and a ceremony and an official
    letter.
When I stand by my mother's grave
it's like saluting
and the hard words of the *Kaddish* a salvo
into the clear summer skies.

We buried her in Sanhedria next to my father's grave,
we kept the place for her
as in a bus or a cinema:
Leaving flowers and stones so no one would take her place.

(Twenty years ago this graveyard was
on the border, facing the enemies' positions.
The tombstones were a good defence against the tanks.)

But in my childhood there was a botanical garden here.
Lots of flowers with frail wooden tags
bearing names of flowers in Hebrew and Latin:
Common Rose, Mediterranean Sage,
Common Scream, Tufted Weeping,
Annual Weeping, Perennial Mourning,
Red Forget-Me-Not, Fragrant Forget-Me-Not,
Forget-me-not, forget.[45]

9

A Festival Garland

With our survey of festival life approaching its end, our *envoi* will bring together a few lines of poetry, old and new, that will constitute a festival garland.

We said earlier (on page 35) that any festival garland had to give pride of place to the poem by Yehuda Amichai which begins 'My mother died on Shavuot when they finished counting the *Omer*.' (The poem appears opposite.) Amichai came to Israel with his family in 1936 at the age of twelve. The poem is magic. A deeply personal experience at one festival, *Shavuot*, becomes in his hands an evocation of history that involves us all.

The crossing-point is in the first line. Counting the *Omer*, as we have seen, is one of numerous ceremonies in the festive year. Now life itself is being counted, and not his mother's life alone.

We shall meet Amichai again at the end of this chapter in a poem that turns another moment in the festive year, the closing service of *Yom Kippur*, into a *mea culpa* that goes to the heart of those who have lived through the Day of Atonement. This closing service, *Ne'ilah*, has an intense personal appeal. The word means literally 'locking up' and gives us the image of 'the gates' – the individual's fate – now being locked up.

Most strikingly, *The Penguin Book of Hebrew Verse* includes a brief, anonymous poem – six lines in Hebrew – ascribed to perhaps the tenth century, which tells us everything of this *Ne'ilah* moment:

Open the Gates

Open the gates to us when the gates
are being closed, for the day is
about to set.

The day shall set, the sun shall go
down and set: let us enter Your
gates.[46]

But there are many ways of responding to *Ne'ilah*. A poem by the greatly gifted Spanish-Jewish poet Moses ibn Ezra (who died in 1135) is more typical of the synagogal style of festival hymn in taking *b'sha'at ha'ne'ilah* ('at the hour of the closing') as a refrain around which he structures eight intricate verses. In Sephardi synagogues, with their special devotion to Spanish-Jewish poetry, the poem is sung as a hymn when the *heichal* (Ark) is opened for the service. A few lines here of a rhymed version in the Sephardi prayer-book illustrate the general approach, though they cannot, of course, convey the skilful intimacy of the rhyming (and allusive) language:

At the Hour of Closing

Lord Almighty, girt with might,
Grant us pardon in thy sight,
        At the closing of the gate.

Mark their hearts out-poured to thee,
Purge their sin: their vanity,
Grant them grace to expiate
        At the closing of the gate.

Michael, prince of Israel,
Eliahu, Gabriel,
Let them cry redemption's date,
        'Tis the closing of the gate.'[47]

In a very different style, we can listen to the *Ne'ilah* thoughts of a young American poet, Lucille Day, in a trilogy of poems on *Yom Kippur* published in a rich anthology called *Voices Within the Ark*:

A Festival Garland

Ne'ilah

Again the day rolls
into darkness; the sky
spills its pinks and purples,
draining to blackness. Deep
inside there is a closing,
a small gate
swinging shut in the mind.
Those few last thoughts
rush through, and a life
is sealed. Outside the temple
a lone bird sounds its call,
waits for response.[48]

'FILLED WITH SONG . . .'

It is a mark of the poetry one hears on festival themes that there is no
ordered 'progress' from the conventional to the 'free', but rather a
persistent presence in all periods of those who break out of the received
style with a voice of their own, so that one is immediately aware of
colour shining out from a mass of writing that is often rather grey.

As far back as the early centuries in which the *tanaim* (*Mishnah*
rabbis) were apparently totally absorbed in legal argument, there was,
in fact, much being written that expressed poetic ideas with as much
personal feeling as one expects to find in 'modern' poetry.

An example that comes to mind to express an overflowing sense of
festival joy is a very ancient poem called *Nishmat* ('The Breath of Life')
that is recited at an early stage in the morning service on the Sabbath
and festivals, starting with a ringing call on every living thing to bless
God's name, and moving on to a rhapsody on life itself:

Though our mouths were full of song as the sea, and our
tongues of exultation as the multitude of its waves,
and our lips of praise as the wide-extended firmament;

though our eyes shone with light like the sun and the moon,
and our hands were spread forth like the eagles
of heaven, and our feet were swift as hinds,

125

we should still be unable to bless God's name for one
thousandth or one ten thousandth part of the bounties
bestowed on our fathers and on us. . . .[49]

In the *Mishnah* period this was known as *birkat ha'shir* ('the blessing in
song'). The rabbis, discussing it, saw it aimed in particular at the
gratitude one feels for every single drop of rain, the source of life. In this
aspect, it is central to the prayers for rain that were so dominant during
the *Sukkot* festival. For good measure the rabbis decided that this
rhapsody should also be part of the *Seder* service on Passover. By now it
had become – and has remained – a familiar and much loved expression
of the underlying happiness that surfaces at festival time.

A MOSES THEME

The imagination was sharpened, perhaps, when festival joy concentrated on a specific drama. If the normal celebration was in measured
verses, full of allusive quotations from the Bible and folklore that make
translation difficult, versifying of a different type has survived here and
there in which the poet asks us to enjoy festival memories in a different
spirit.

There is a lively example of this in a long, free-wheeling poem of the
tenth century, which takes off from the triumphs of Israel in crossing
the Red Sea and is designed, therefore, to be read in the service of the
seventh day of Passover, when the Bible reading covers this drama.

The poet, Moses ben Kalonymus, was a member of a famed literary
family that made its way, under the protection of one of the Carolingian
emperors, from North Italy to the Rhineland, which perhaps provided
a double background to his inspiration. His imagination is certainly
phenomenally rich in detail in its Technicolor evocation of Pharaoh's
pursuit of the Israelites. At one point he talks of the fiery steeds that
God sent out on the Red Sea to lure the Egyptian charioteers to their
fate. At another, we hear of the epic battle between the Prince of the Sea
(protective angel of Israel) and the Prince or angel of Egypt. It is with a
happy touch that he brings us back at the end to the maidens singing
their song of triumph, as in the Bible, under the guidance of Moses's
sister Miriam.

The brief extract here is from a long *kerova* (prayer insertion) to be chanted in synagogue:

Pharaoh Pursues the Israelites

And the glory of the Lord God of Israel appeared among the multitude of legions. Riding on a cherub, He swooped down upon the men of strife. In his company were the seraphim, the holy creatures, the ofanim, and thousands upon thousands, myriads upon myriads of angelic troops, with fiery chariots, fiery horses, and all the other apparitions which the prophet beheld in his ecstatic vision: red horses, and black, sorrel and white. Then they camped opposite each other, wheels ready to roll, face to face: an army of fire and an army of straw.

Then the Prince of the Sea and the Prince of Egypt came to grips, struggling with each other in the heavens. Rahav, the Prince of the Sea, with the help of the Chariot-Dweller, overpowered the Prince of the Egyptians, hurled him down to earth and trampled him.

And when the Israelites witnessed these judgements, how the protector and those he protected met their doom, they shouted and sang songs of praise. The singers went first, then came the musicians, and among them maidens playing timbrels. Only afterwards were the angels permitted to sing.[50]

If Moses is in the background in this particular Passover celebration, he is very much in the foreground in Jewish festival legend generally, and treated occasionally in a style less portentous than in the Kalonymus extravaganza. A particularly unexpected treatment emerges in a very long poetical sequence on the death of Moses that turns reverence into a kind of folk-song. T. Carmi, the editor of *The Penguin Book of Hebrew Verse*, where this surprising sequence appears, helps us to understand, in a scholarly note, how strong the flow of instinctual poetry of this kind must have been in the Middle Ages.[51] The extracts he gives are, he says, only an abridgement of what was composed by various hands in the eighth to the eleventh cnturies and then published in the sixteenth century as part of the liturgy of *Simchat Torah*, the festival which celebrates the rejoicing over the Torah as part of *Sukkot* (see page 87).

Nothing could be more apt than applying a sequence of this kind – totally reverential and at the same time totally playful – to the spirit of *Simchat Torah*. Unless one recognizes this mixture, one misses the underlying flavour of all the festivals. To celebrate the Jewish faith is not a commitment to legalism or pomposity. If anything, it is a commitment to the intellectual liveliness that has fuelled Jewish life in all the ages.

This multi-authored sequence brings it all to life in the style of Jewish non-stop arguments. We start with the angels objecting that Moses should never have been allowed to ascend to heaven and take the Torah away. We then find Moses in endless argument with God, determined to get answers to what is unanswerable: why has he to die, and how? His mother appears in Egypt searching for his grave. It is folklore that is alive in every word, and as much today as a thousand years ago when it was written.

Some of the stanzas have indeed become folksongs in their own right, like the first (*mi alah la-marom*) which begins:

> Who went up to heaven?
> Who went up to heaven?
> Who went up to heaven, and brought
> > down the mighty mainstay?

'How then shall I die?' Moses asks God at one stage. God replies:

> By My own self I swear:
> You shall hear me say:
> 'May your soul be treasured
> > in the treasury of life:
> And you shall not dje as all men die.'

To find this in the *Simchat Torah* prayer-book is one more illustration of the wide range of experience that (as we saw earlier) is released in *Sukkot* ceremonies. Two days before *Simchat Torah*, the congregants will have been flourishing their palm branches as they called out the *hosha'anahs* of *Hosha'anah Rabbah*. In extracts which follow from a long poem by a young American poet, Sol Lachman, we see how the palms fire his imagination, as he thinks of Jewish history in the *Sukkot* framework:

128

We waited in the desert encircled
for the vessel of years to be filled
in circles of tents and hasty enclosures

. . . We hang red fruits from the rafter
crush red seeds in our mouths
running sweet and wet

. . . we shake the palm branch
& it rustles loud in each of the four corners

we have lived in corners
& feared the rustling of every branch

now we face the wind & we shout
& we shake our branch in all directions
& the wind is cedar boughs and citron
& the harvest is clear & sweet on our tongues
& even the birds are made joyful
by our shouts[52]

A SPECIAL *PURIM*

It is heartening to hear a response of joy when for many young poets
Jewish history is a tale of woe: 'we have lived in corners'. The
alternation is familiar; but in times like the present, when a horror
without equal still permeates all Jewish feeling, it sometimes needs a
special will to recall the many earlier deliverances, as magical in their
impact as the original deliverance celebrated by *Purim*.

There are always dangers lurking; and from early times a special
additional *Purim* became a regular holiday, celebrated in full *Purim*-
style, whenever a community or family was saved from the brink. In
many cases, an almost exact parallel was experienced, with a new
Haman exposed, defeated and even executed, as in the Esther story.

The magisterial *Encyclopaedia Judaica* of 1972 gives a list of 101 places
where a Special *Purim* was instituted, and names eleven families who
instituted a celebration of their own family deliverance.[53] We see from
the detail given that the earliest Special *Purim* was in 1191 at Breche

(Champagne, France), close in time and place to the background of Rashi, one of the greatest scholars of the Middle Ages.

At Brèche, we are told, 'the chief Jew-baiter was executed'. In Castille, in 1339, the *Purim* parallel is very close: 'the Jews were saved from annihilation following accusations by the Jew-baiter Gonzales Martinez, the king's adviser'. At Frankfurt, in 1616, the Jews who had been expelled from the town were readmitted, with the chief Jew-baiter, Fettemilch, executed. Among family *Purims*, we read of 'the Plum Jam *Purim*' of 1731 in a small Bohemian town, when David Brandeis and his family were saved from the accusation of having killed gentiles by poisoning plum jam.

But there is one eloquent record of the origins of a Special *Purim* that dwarfs all these deliverances, not only in its literary detail but in its spirit of exaltation that adds up to a festival celebration of life itself.

The writer concerned, Samuel Ha-Nagid ('the Prince'), was a poet and general of southern Spain who dominated the world in which he lived in the first half of the eleventh century. Born in Cordoba and enjoying the most sophisticated Jewish and general education there when it was the capital of the Caliphate, he had had to flee at the age of twenty, following an invasion of wild Berber hordes. During the ensuing twenty-five years he became celebrated as a remarkable talmudist and poet, as illustrated in the rare distinction of his title 'Ha-Nagid' ('the Prince'). But astonishingly he was at the same time developing outstanding military skills, which led to his appointment in 1038 as vizier and general to the armies of the Berber ruler, now established in Granada. It was not enough that Samuel led the Berber armies to a series of victories in campaigns against Seville and its allies; the truly rewarding thing for Jewish literature was that he recorded his adventures, military and personal, in an unending flow of Hebrew poems that constitute a diary of his stormy life.[54]

Given his background, it is not surprising that even a straight military account of a battle against Seville is told with Jewish imagery. In one long poem-report of 1039, designed to be inserted as a thanksgiving ode into a festival service, he rejoices that he has been able to defeat Isma'il ibn Abbad, commander of the Seville armies, who had planned to destroy the Jewish community of Granada. To Samuel, it is like Israel's victory in the Wilderness over the traditional enemy Amalek. His poem therefore called for a Special *Purim* to be declared:

Now the traces of Amalek were wiped out
from Spain, and their enemies destroyed,
as once before when Agag perished at the
hand of Samuel, and Haman by Mordecai. . . .

Now make a second *Purim* for the God who
cut off from Amalek flower and fruit, and make
it heard in Africa and Egypt, and notify the
children of the chosen house

And tell it to the elders of Pumbeditha, and
to the sages of the academy at Sura, and
call its name:
   'Sister to the Happening of Ahashverosh and Lady Esther'
and write it in your books that it may abide
forever and be remembered from generation
   to generation.

In another victory, the celebration is to be relived through the
adjacent feast of *Sukkot*:

In the month of the Mighty Ones you gave
   your servant to drink the cup of salvation. . . .

There was light for me on the eve of the festival
   of Harvest Gathering. . . .
I observed properly the Lord's festivals
As was the practice among the Dwellers in
   Tents . . . .
Even the Sabbath days and the day of the
   Shofar and Atonement
The days of the *Sukkah* until the exit of
   the pilgrims

At the time the people brought into their booths
Myrtle from the rock and branches from
   the palm tree
The Rock exalted me with the palm of His hand
And His Booth was my shelter
   like a sealed-up fortress. . . .

131

THE ANSWER AT *NE'ILAH*

For Samuel, the exultation of *Sukkot* had been based on '*Shofar* and Atonement'. He had shared, as all do, the intimacy of the closing service of *Yom Kippur*, *Ne'ilah*, the hour when 'the gates are locked'.

Among contemporary poets, it is a theme which imposes itself almost against their will. Jack Myers, an American, expresses his personal anguish when he asks, in a poem on *Yom Kippur*, what sin amounts to for his generation:

> a few faces bright with guilt
> went up against the wind
> and fell like sinful children
> without a splash

Life is drained of meaning in a struggle to win. At the end of the twenty-four-hour fast, 'the emptiness that drilled us out has hungered'. When God is brought down to earth, 'it changes the taste of the sea'.[55]

Yehuda Amichai, writing in Hebrew of thoughts that surfaced for him at *Ne'ilah*, broadens his response to fit the scene in which he lives. As with the poem we read earlier on *Shavuot*, there is an extra dimension to be confronted in Israel. In differing ways both Arabs and Jews face a locking of the gates. The whole poem has to be read:

> *On Yom Kippur*
>
> On Yom Kippur in 1967
> I put on my dark holiday suit and went into
>   the Old City in Jerusalem.
> For a long time I stood in the niche
>   of an Arab's shop
> Not far from the Nablus Gate, a shop
> Of buttons and zippers and rolls of thread
> In all colours, and snaps and buckles.
> A glorious light and a great many colours
>   like a Holy Ark with its doors ajar.
>
> I told him in my heart that my father too
> Had a shop like this of threads and buttons.

I explained to him in my heart all about the
    tens of years
And the reasons and the events that I
    am now here
And my father's shop is in ashes there, and he is
    buried here.

By the time I had finished it was the hour of
    Ne'ilah.
He too pulled down the shutter and locked
    the gate.
And I went back home with all the worshippers.[56]

THE FIVE *MEGILLOT*

It is not surprising that our festival garland has ranged beyond the simple rejoicing that each celebration might have seemed to call for. We would have found the same many-sided expression of Jewish life if we had sought to include in our garland some words from the *megillot*, the five Bible books – *Esther, Ruth, Lamentations, Ecclesiastes* and the *Song of Songs* – specifically chosen to be read as a kind of literary treat at the festivals. In some cases, the link of one of the books with a particular festival is very obvious, as, for example, the book of *Esther* with *Purim*. In other cases – say *Ecclesiastes* with *Sukkot* – no link is particularly visible, but this, far from being a puzzle, opens up a different way of looking at the meaning that lies in the choice of these books. Supplementing any direct link with the festivals, the wide range of subject-matter in these books illustrates perfectly the many-sided diversity of Jewish experience, which one explores with particular satisfaction in the relaxed ambience of a festival mood.

Each of the books in question is a masterly work of art, complete in itself and quite separate in tone from the integrated intensity of the Bible as a whole. The major Bible books and the religious rituals carried out during the festivals are designed to inculcate an established view. The variety of the *megillot* means that we are confronted with more than one theme and find ourselves carried forward in this spirit.

Each book, then, has a place in our festival garland. In one mood we are ready to enjoy *Ruth* and *Esther* as brilliant novellas; in another we are moved beyond words by the plangent strophes of *Lamentations*. With the *Song of Songs* we applaud the readiness of the rabbis to admit a joyous love story into the official Bible canon, even though they purported to approve it only as an allegory. It was with equal daring that they admitted *Ecclesiastes*, almost a counter-culture to official piety, though with a half-suggestion that the sophisticated scepticism expressed so elegantly in this book can sit comfortably with faith as part of the good life.

We can look back to Amichai's poem for the last word. In all his poetry he expresses a unity in Jewish experience that overrides its diversity. When the arguments are over, we go 'back home', as he says, 'with all the worshippers'.

Reference Notes

1 Josephus, *Jewish Antiquities*, vol. IV, paras 203–4
2 Josephus, *The Jewish War*, vol. VI, para. 425
3 Salo Baron in the *Encyclopaedia Judaica*, vol. 13, col. 871
4 Philo, *On the Special Laws*, 1:59
5 Josephus, *Jewish Antiquities*, vol. VIII, paras 311–12
6 *Bikkurim*, 3:2–4
7 Josephus, *Jewish Antiquities*, vol. XIII, para. 372
8 *Aboth*, 5:5
9 *Ecclesiasticus* (Apocrypha), 45:6–10
10 *Midrash on Lamentations*, v:18, in Chaim Raphael, *The Walls of Jerusalem* (1968), pp.202–3
11 *Sukkot*, 1:9
12 *Rosh Hashanah*, 1:2
13 Yigael Yadin, *Bar Kokhba* (1971), p.129
14 Isadore Twersky, *A Maimonides Reader* (1972), p.2*ff*
15 Franz Kobler (ed.), *Letters of Jews Through the Ages*, 2 vols. (1953), pp.297*ff*
16 *Rosh Hashanah*, 17a
17 Josephus, *The Jewish War*, vol. II, para. 184*ff*
18 John B. Pritchard (ed.), *Ancient Near Eastern Texts Relating to the Old Testament* (1969)
19 William Foxwell Albright, *Yahweh and the Gods of Canaan* (1968), p.180
20 *Ibid.*, p.175
21 Theodore H. Gaster, *Myth, Legend and Custom in the Old Testament* (1969), p.632*ff*
22 S. H. Hooke, *Myth, Ritual and Kingship* (1958), p.19
23 Gaster, *op. cit.*, p.747
24 *Rosh Hashanah*, sections 1–3 for the quotations which follow
25 *Midrash Genesis Rabbah*, 6:3
26 Theodore H. Gaster, *Festivals of the Jewish Year* (1953), p.33
27 *Pesahim*, section 10
28 For a full discussion, see Herman Kieval, 'The Curious Case of *Kol Nidre*', *Commentary* (US), October 1968, pp.53–8
29 *Ta'anit*, 4:8
30 Josephus, *Jewish Antiquities*, vol. XII, para. 325
31 Israel Abrahams, *Festival Studies* (1906), p.146

32 Irene Awret, *Days of Honey* (1984), pp.41–9

33 Chaim Raphael, *A Feast of History* (1972), p.168

34 Beth-Zion Abrahams (tr. from original Yiddish and ed.), *The Life of Glückel of Hameln, 1646–1724: Written by Herself* (1962)

35 S. V. Agnon, *The Bridal Canopy* (tr. I. M. Lask, 1967), pp.68–76

36 Cecil Roth, *A History of the Marranos* (1932), pp.168–82

37 Seymour B. Liebman, *New World Jewry, 1493–1825* (1982)

38 Roth, *op. cit.*, pp.159–60

39 Kobler (ed.) *op. cit.*, vol. II, pp.480–85

40 Shmarya Levin, *Forward from Exile* (ed. Maurice Samuel, 1967)

41 Abraham I. Katsh (tr. and ed.), *Scroll of Agony: Warsaw Diary of Chaim A. Kaplan* (1965)

42 Antony Polonsky (ed.), *A Cup of Tears: A Diary of the Warsaw Ghetto* (1988)

43 Teddy Kollek, *For Jerusalem: A Life* (1978), p.187

44 *Ibid.*, p.197

45 *Tel Aviv Review*, January 1988, vol. I, p.16

46 T. Carmi (ed.), *The Penguin Book of Hebrew Verse* (1981), p.241

47 The Sephardi prayer-book has taken this version by Herbert Loewe from his charming book *Mediaeval Hebrew Minstrelsy* (1926), p.119

48 Howard Schwartz and Anthony Rudolf (eds), *Voices Within the Ark* (1980), p.446

49 S. Singer (ed.), *Prayer Book* (1935), pp.125–6

50 Carmi (ed.), *op. cit.*, pp.260–62

51 *Ibid.*, pp.95–6. The full sequence is set out on pp.266–74

52 Schwartz and Rudolf (eds), *op. cit.*, p.562

53 *Encyclopaedia Judaica* (1972), vol. 13, cols 1395–1400

54 Leon J. Weinberger (tr. and ed.), *Jewish Prince in Moslem Spain: Selected Poems of Samuel ibn Nagrela* (1973). The verses quoted here are, in the English version, on pp. 26–8 and 39–41 respectively.

55 Schwartz and Rudolf (eds), *op. cit.*, p.562

56 *Ibid.*, p.29, with slight adaptations.

Acknowledgements and Bibliography

The author is grateful to Yehuda Amichai for permission to print his poems on pages 122 and 132, and to Lucille Day for her poem on page 125. The poems on pages 124 and 127 are reproduced by permission of Penguin Books Ltd from *The Penguin Book of Hebrew Verse*, edited by T. Carmi (1981), pages 241 and 261. Brief extracts from *The Bridal Canopy* by S. V. Agnon and from *Days of Honey* by Irene Awret are given with kind permission of Schocken Books. Brief extracts from *Glückel of Hameln* and from *Letters of Jews Through the Ages* are with kind permission of the publishers, formerly East and West Library of London and now The Hebrew Publishing Company, Brooklyn, New York. Thanks are due to the joint editors, Howard Schwartz and Anthony Rudolf, for help in tracking and clearing poems in their anthology *Voices Within the Ark*, and to the Jewish Publication Society of America for permission to draw on Shmarya Levin's *Forward from Exile*. It is good to acknowledge with thanks brief quotations from the poems of Samuel ibn Nagrela in Leon J. Weinberger's *Jewish Prince in Moslem Spain* (University of Alabama Press, 1973), and the Marrano information in *New World Jewry 1493–1825* by Seymour B. Liebman (Ktav, 1982). The brief and sad extracts from *Scroll of Agony*, edited by Abraham I. Katsh (Hamish Hamilton Ltd), and from *A Cup of Tears*, edited by Antony Polonsky (Basil Blackwell Ltd), are acknowledged with thanks, as are the happy references in *For Jerusalem: A Life* by Teddy Kollek, published by Weidenfeld and Nicolson. The author is grateful as before to Linda Osband for her resourceful and sympathetic editing; and to Andrea Stern for her very skilful work on the illustrations.

FESTIVAL PRAYERS AND TRANSLATIONS
Transliteration of Hebrew words throughout is in familiar style for simplicity.

The full service for *Rosh Hashanah* and *Yom Kippur* is given in *Service of the Synagogue* (Ashkenazi form), 3 vols (Routledge, 1906); and *The Book of Prayer*, vols 2 and 3 (Spanish and Portuguese form) (Oxford, 1961).

A very full presentation of festival anthems, in rhymed form, is given in *The*

Acknowledgements and Bibliography

Traditional Prayer Book for Sabbath and Festivals, edited and translated by David de Sola Pool (Behrman House, New York, 1960). This includes the famed anthem *Akdamut* (pp.505–12).

A BRIEF LIST OF BOOKS DRAWN ON HERE

Beth-Zion Abrahams (tr. and ed.), *The Life of Glückel of Hameln, 1646–1724: Written by Herself* (1962)

Israel Abrahams; *Festival Studies* (1906)

S. V. Agnon, *The Bridal Canopy* (1967)

Robert Alter and Frank Kermode (eds), *The Literary Guide to the Bible* (1987)

Yehuda Amichai, *Selected Poems* (1988)

Irene Awret, *Days of Honey* (1984)

T. Carmi (ed.), *The Penguin Book of Hebrew Verse* (1981)

Herbert Danby, *The Mishnah* (1933)

Theodore H. Gaster, *Myth, Legend and Custom in the Old Testament* (1969)

David Goldstein, *Jewish Folklore and Legend* (1980)

Judah Halevi, *Selected Poems* (tr. Nina Salaman, 1928)

Josephus, *Jewish Antiquities* (ed. Thackeray, 1930)

Josephus, *The Jewish War* (ed. Thackeray, 1928)

Abraham I. Katsh (ed.), *Scroll of Agony: Warsaw Diary of Chaim A. Kaplan* (1965)

Franz Kobler (ed.), *Letters of Jews Through the Ages*, 2 vols (1953)

Teddy Kollek, *For Jerusalem* (1978)

Shmarya Levin, *Forward from Exile* (ed. Maurice Samuel, 1967)

Seymour B. Liebman, *New World Jewry, 1493–1825* (1982)

Anthony Polonsky (ed.), *A Cup of Tears: A Diary of the Warsaw Ghetto* (1988)

Chaim Raphael, *A Feast of History* (1972)

Cecil Roth, *A History of the Marranos* (1932)

Howard Schwartz and Anthony Rudolf (eds), *Voices Within the Ark* (1980)

Leon J. Weinberger (tr. and ed.), *Jewish Prince in Moslem Spain: Selected Poems of Samuel ibn Nagrela* (1973)

Yigael Yadin, *Bar Kokhba* (1971)

Mark Zborowski and Elizabeth Herzog, *Life is with People: The Culture of the Shtetl* (1962)

Index